CAMPAIGN 400

SECOND PUNIC WAR IN IBERIA 220–206 BC

From Hannibal at the Tagus to the Battle of Ilipa

MIR BAHMANYAR　　ILLUSTRATED BY MARCO CAPPARONI

OSPREY PUBLISHING
Bloomsbury Publishing Plc
Kemp House, Chawley Park, Cumnor Hill, Oxford OX2 9PH, UK
29 Earlsfort Terrace, Dublin 2, Ireland
1385 Broadway, 5th Floor, New York, NY 10018, USA
E-mail: info@ospreypublishing.com
www.ospreypublishing.com

OSPREY is a trademark of Osprey Publishing Ltd

First published in Great Britain in 2024

© Osprey Publishing Ltd, 2024

A catalogue record for this book is available from the British Library.

ISBN: PB 9781472859754; eBook 9781472859747; ePDF 9781472859730;
XML 9781472859723

24 25 26 27 28 10 9 8 7 6 5 4 3 2 1

Maps by Bounford.com
3D BEVs by Paul Kime
Index by Sharon Redmayne
Typeset by PDQ Digital Media Solutions, Bungay, UK
Printed and bound in India by Replika Press Private Ltd.

To find out more about our authors and books visit
www.ospreypublishing.com. Here you will find extracts, author
interviews, details of forthcoming events and the option to sign up for
our newsletter.

Osprey Publishing supports the Woodland Trust, the UK's leading woodland
conservation charity.

Artist's note

Readers may care to note that the original paintings from which the colour
plates in this book were prepared are available for private sale. All
reproduction copyright whatsoever is retained by the publishers. All
enquiries should be addressed to the artist via the below website:

https://marcocapparoni.com/

The publishers regret that they can enter into no correspondence upon
this matter.

Photographic images

Unless otherwise indicated, the photographs that appear in this work are in
the public domain.

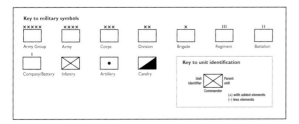

Front cover main illustration: The Battle of the Upper Baetis, near
Ilorca, 211 BC. (Marco Capparoni)

Title page photograph: A coin showing the head of
Hasdrubal Barca.

CONTENTS

The Iberian Peninsula during the Second Punic War

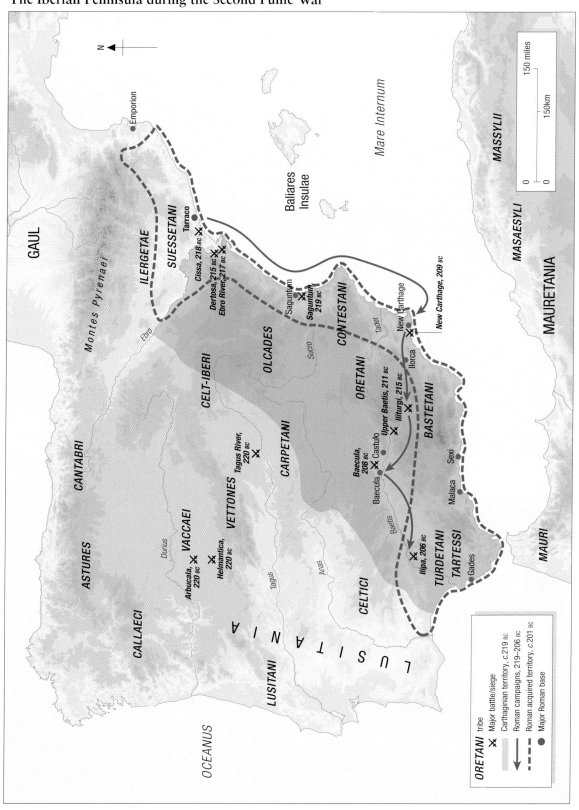

GAUL

Emporion

Montes Pyrenaei

ILERGETAE

SUESSETANI

Tarraco

Cissa, 218 BC

Dertosa, 215 BC
Ebro River, 217 BC

Ebro

CELT-IBERI

OLCADES

Saguntum

Saguntum,
219 BC

Sucro

CONTESTANI

Tader

New Carthage

New Carthage, 209 BC

Ilorca

Upper Baetis, 211 BC

ORETANI

Iliturgi, 215 BC

BASTETANI

CANTABRI

CARPETANI

VETTONES

Tagus River,
220 BC

Baecula,
208 BC

Castulo

Baecula

Baetis

Sexi

ASTURES

VACCAEI

Durius

Arbucala,
220 BC

Helmantica,
220 BC

Tagus

Anas

Malaca

TURDETANI

TARTESSI

Ilipa, 206 BC

Gades

CALLAECI

CELTICI

L U S I T A N I A

OCEANUS

LUSITANI

Mare Internum

Baliares
Insulae

MASSYLII

MASAESYLI

MAURETANIA

MAURI

N

150 miles

150km

0

0

ORETANI tribe

✗ Major battle/siege

Carthaginian territory, c.219 BC

Roman campaigns, 219–206 BC

Roman acquired territory, c.201 BC

● Major Roman base

INTRODUCTION

The contest for the Western Mediterranean between Carthage and Rome stretched over three wars and 120 years, of which 44 were spent in combat. These wars, collectively known as the Punic Wars (264–146 BC), ended with the destruction of Carthage.[1] These comprise one of the longest continuous wars in history, and arguably the greatest conflict in Roman history. They resulted in a new era in Europe and a new unity of ancient history focusing on Rome until its division into two halves in the 3rd century AD. No other states or nations, wrote ancient Roman historian Livy (59 BC to AD 17), that have come into conflict had greater resources than these two peoples, nor had the combatants themselves ever been so powerful.

The story of Rome and Carthage is rooted in the mythology of a bittersweet love story detailed in the *Aeneid* by Roman poet Publius Vergilius Maro, better known as Virgil (70–19 BC). Both cities were founded by refugees. Queen Elissa, also known as Dido, fled the Phoenician Semitic city of Tyre (80km south of Beirut, Lebanon) upon her wealthy husband's murder

---

1   The word 'Punic' comes from the word 'Phoenician' (*punicus* in Latin), and is used to refer to the Carthaginians, who were descendants of the Phoenicians. The terms 'Punic' and 'Carthaginian' are used interchangeably throughout this work.

Dido orders oxhide cut into strips to lay out the foundation of her new city Qart-ḥadašt (Carthage) centred around the hill of Byrsa. The word 'Byrsa' is rooted in the Greek for oxhide. (NY Public Library)

The Death of Dido by Belgian artist Joseph Stallaert (1825–1903), painted around 1872.

by her brother Pygmalion. Initially, she and her companions sailed to Cyprus around 825 BC, but Elissa settled along the coast of North Africa in 814 BC, where she founded Qart-ḥadašt (or Carthage). A local Berber king allowed the queen to establish a new home, but it had to fit within the hide of an ox. Elissa ordered the hide cut into thin strips, centred around a hilltop called the Byrsa overlooking a natural harbour in the Gulf of Tunis, and Carthage was born.

Into the city of Carthage, borne on a fierce storm, arrived the handsome warrior Aeneas, who had survived the sacking of Troy by the Greeks. He, too, sought a new place to call home, having already failed in Sicily. After a torrid love affair with Elissa, who believed she had found her soulmate, a marriage was proposed that allowed joint rule, but Aeneas fled in 759 BC to Sicily, to eventually land in Latium, Italy, where his descendants founded Rome. Angered by his betrayal, Queen Elissa uttered curses of eternal hatred before killing herself with a sword Aeneas had given her as a present. Elissa's curses set the course for an inevitable war with Rome.

Rome was founded in 753 BC on one of seven hills, and its origins, too, are shrouded in a myth best detailed by the Greek historian and later Roman citizen Plutarch (AD 46–120). Plutarch writes of Rome's founding brothers Romulus and Remus, both descendants of the god Mars and Rhea Silvia (herself a descendant of Aeneas), who were suckled by a she-wolf and fed by a woodpecker before being adopted by a shepherd and his wife. The boys' names derive from the Latin word for teat (*ruma*). During a disagreement about the location of the new city, Romulus killed his brother. Thus, Rome was founded. Plutarch notes: 'Romulus divided all the multitude that were of age to bear arms into military companies, each company consisting of 3,000 footmen and 300 horsemen. Such a company was called a "legion", because the warlike were selected out of all.'

These foundation legends set a grand stage for the bitter and passionate wars between the descendants of the refugees Elissa and Aeneas. Despite three treaties (in 509, 348 and 306 BC) acknowledging the other's hegemonies, the Punic Wars engulfed Carthage and Rome. The titanic struggle spanned over 100 years and was fought to the bitter end between equal rivals.

The Punic Wars pitted a nation of Roman farmers against Carthaginian traders – but it was not merely a war between the two powers; the conflict, which had three distinct phases, involved numerous tribes, cultures and territories. The First Punic War, starting in 264 BC, had its roots in Sicily. Mercenaries (the Mamertines) had seized the Greek city of Messina in 288 BC on the north-eastern part of the island during the Greco-Punic War (580–265 BC), but were defeated by the Greek cities led by Syracuse. The Mamertines asked for assistance from Carthage when they found themselves besieged by Hiero II of Syracuse (308–215 BC), only to reach out to the Romans for support against their former Punic allies. This resulted in a prolonged war for hegemony over Sicily pitting Punic, Roman and Greek forces against one another. By 247 BC, Carthage was facing defeat when Hamilcar Barca was appointed commander of the Sicilian campaign. Although Hamilcar remained undefeated, he was unable to overturn Roman advantages. The First Punic War ended in 241 BC, leaving Carthage defeated and its former naval supremacy in pieces, supplanted by victorious Rome. The peace treaty expelled Carthage from Sicily, required the withdrawal of Punic forces and exacted an indemnity of 1,000 talents immediately with an additional 2,200 talents, roughly 56 tons of silver, to be paid over ten years, ending in 231/230 BC.

A Phoenician pendant in translucent deep colbalt blue, with suspension ring in the same colour and applied decoration in opaque yellow and white. This belongs to a group of head pendants with oriental features that appears to have been made in Phoenicia and Cyprus, as well as at Carthage in North Africa. (The Metropolitan Museum of Art)

Punic mercenaries were transported to North Africa, where unpaid wages led to a brutal war in 240 BC, with some natives joining the rebellion and nearly destroying Carthage. In around 237 BC, after horrific violence, the Truceless War ended under Hamilcar Barca's leadership. During the war for survival, Rome had at first stood by Carthage only to then renege on the terms of its treaty, exploiting Carthage's weakness by seizing several islands, including Sardinia and Corsica. Rome also demanded an additional 1,200 talents in reparations.

Following its expansion into the Iberian Peninsula, Carthage was able to rise from the ashes of two brutal wars. The shadow of the First Punic War and Roman bad faith during the Truceless War led to a complicated relationship between the two powers. Both were expanding, suppressing revolts and weaving alliances throughout the Mediterranean basin. Massilia (Marseilles, France), a Greek colony, felt its trade and hegemony threatened by Carthaginian encroachment in south-eastern Spain. Continuous complaints to Rome eventually led to envoys seeking clarifications from Punic leaders with an understanding that the Ebro River was to form the boundary of Carthaginian expansion. However, one of Massilia's trading partners was the fortified city of Saguntum (Arse, now modern Sagunto), well south of the river. Roman interference, coupled with the murder of pro-Carthaginian supporters, led to Hannibal, then commander of Punic Spain, laying siege to and capturing the city after a gruelling eight months. Saguntum became, like Messina of Sicily, the trigger for war. Roman envoys declared war to the Carthaginian senate in

A late 19th-century depiction of Carthaginian merchants at a Roman villa, who could be selling a slave.

218 BC. This second of three wars, the subject of this work, ended in 202 BC with another Roman victory; however, it had nearly ruined Rome.

Despite the agreement of a peace treaty, the Third Punic War broke out in 149 BC, to shouts of 'Carthage must be destroyed' echoing in the chambers of the Roman Senate uttered by the fanatical Second Punic War veteran Cato the Elder (234–149 BC). The trigger came when Rome falsely accused Carthage of having broken the treaty by suppressing a Numidian revolt. It ended three years later with the final destruction of Carthage, the population of which was put to the sword or taken into slavery.

ORIGINS OF THE IBERIAN CAMPAIGN: 247–221 BC

By 247 BC, Carthage was losing the First Punic War raging in Sicily. That same year, Hamilcar Barca (at the age of 28) was appointed commander of Punic forces on the island. His son Hannibal was born around this time and would be absent from Carthage for 36 years by the time he returned in 202 BC. Although Hamilcar remained undefeated by waging primarily a guerrilla war, he was unable to turn the tide, only retaining the cities of Lilybaeum and Drepana on the western edge of Sicily. Carthage ordered him to negotiate terms with Rome, thus ending the war. Punic forces vacated Sicily and relocated to North Africa.

Mercenary veterans of the Sicilian campaign revolted as payments by Carthage were slow in coming. These veterans were joined by native tribes, and the Truceless War broke out in North Africa. It featured such brutality that even ancient sources, long accustomed to violence, mention its depravity. Around 237 BC, Hamilcar successfully quashed the mercenary revolt, while at the same time Rome exploited Carthage's hardships by forcing it to surrender Sardinia, Corsica and other smaller islands in the Western Mediterranean, despite the 509 BC treaty recognizing Carthage's dominion over them. To add salt to the wound, Rome exacted 1,200 talents in reparations, to be paid immediately.

Despite these setbacks, Carthage drove its expansion westwards away from Roman interference. Hamilcar's task was to recover former colonies in Iberia, and to expand beyond the limited locations along its well-established coastal trading routes and the mining sites primarily in the south-eastern region of modern Andalucia. Hamilcar, accompanied by his sons Hannibal (aged 9), Hasdrubal (7) and Mago (5), and his son-in-law Hasdrubal the Fair, set off in 237 BC for Gadir (Gadeira at the Pillars of Heracles, modern Cadiz) in southern Spain. Hamilcar's army marched along the shores of North Africa accompanied at sea by Hasdrubal the Fair's naval forces. Crossing into Iberia, Gadir became the base for expansion into the south-east of the peninsula. Iberia in the 3rd century BC, especially in its valleys, was 'thickly wooded with holm oak-related species'. It was not the treeless country we see today.

In 236 BC, Hamilcar waged war on the Tartessians (Turdetani/Turduli) led by Istolatius and his brother in the valley of the Baetis (modern Guadalquivir River). The Iberians were defeated, with both brothers killed in battle. Three thousand survivors were absorbed into the Carthaginian army. Hamilcar then faced another force, this time an army of 50,000 men, raised by the native leader Indortes. But before the actual fighting even began, Indortes fled to a hill, perhaps a fortified settlement, where Hamilcar laid siege. Attempting to flee under the cover of darkness, Indortes was captured and many of his men were killed. After putting out his eyes and maltreating his person, Hamilcar had him crucified; but the rest of the prisoners, numbering more than 10,000, were released. Hamilcar then won over many cities by diplomacy and others by force of arms. These victories allowed for Punic expansion into eastern Iberia, whereas previously Carthage's control was limited to the southern shores.

Sometime between 237 and 236 BC, Hamilcar ordered Hasdrubal the Fair and his army to North Africa to crush a Numidian revolt. Hasdrubal was successful, killing 8,000 and capturing 2,000 prisoners.

In 231 BC, Hamilcar founded the city of Acra Leuce (perhaps Alicante) near the rivers of the Baetis and Tader, which was considered a secure area under Carthaginian control. That same year, Roman envoys sought answers on behalf of the Greek colony and Roman ally Massilia, which was troubled by Punic advances interrupting previously established trade with peoples and Greek colonies along the south-eastern seaboard of the peninsula. When asked about his intentions, Hamilcar answered the envoys that everything served to honour the treaty by paying off the large war indemnities owed to Rome. It is interesting to note that the reparations should already have been paid off by this point.

While besieging the town of Helike (perhaps Elche de la Sierra, 160km east of Acra Leuce) in 228 BC, Hamilcar sent most of his army and elephants to his headquarters at Acra Leuce to quarter for the approaching winter season. Betrayed by the proffered friendship of King Orisos of the Orrisi (the Oretani, according to the Greek historian Strabo) during the siege, Hamilcar Barca was ambushed and killed in battle. Hamilcar's death remains a mystery, as another ancient source, the Greek historian Diodorus Siculus (writing in the 1st century BC), mentions death by drowning: 'In the course of his flight Hamilcar contrived to save the lives of his sons and his friends by turning aside on another road; overtaken by the king, he plunged on horseback into a large river and perished in the flood under his steed, but his sons Hannibal and Hasdrubal made their way safely to Acra Leuce.'

An 1862 illustration from *Salammbo*, written by Gustave Flaubert (1821–80), by the French illustrator and cartoonist Victor-Armand Poirson (1858–93) showing Spendius, the former slave of Hamilcar turned leader of the mercenary revolt, with possibly the Libyan prince Matho, leader of the mercenaries during the Truceless War.

Another illustration by Poirson for Flaubert's *Salammbo,* showing the crucifixion of mercenary leaders during the Truceless War.

In Hamilcar's nine-year rule, he subjugated native tribes and laid the foundation for the Punic empire in the Iberian Peninsula. Resources acquired primarily from silver mining, along with the manpower additions of Iberians and Celt-Iberians to the army, restored Carthage's prosperity after its earlier devastating wars. By the time of his death, Hamilcar Barca's army was composed of Celt-Iberians, Iberians and a backbone of African troops, and officered by veteran Carthaginian commanders, making this the best Carthaginian land army to date.

Much has been written about Hamilcar's hatred of Rome, which even featured making Hannibal swear an oath of eternal enmity to it, but it is doubtful that Hamilcar sought to wage a war with Rome, even though it had been deceitful with the seizure of key islands and demanding reparations amid the desperate struggle of the Truceless War. Arguments have been made that his control of southern Iberia, along with its mineral and agricultural wealth, created a base for a future war against Rome. However, it is not unreasonable to suggest that Hamilcar's success in Spain would not have caused him or Carthage to desire another war. No single man controlled or could control geopolitical machinations or an entire war, not Hamilcar and not even the great Hannibal.

After Hamilcar's death, his son-in-law Hasdrubal the Fair became the commander of the Punic-Iberian forces from 228 to 211 BC. He further expanded Carthaginian control sometimes by diplomacy and sometimes by war. Hasdrubal the Fair first crushed the treacherous Orrisi/Oretani, who were responsible for Hamilcar's death, and seized 12 of their cities. He then married the daughter of an Iberian king and established relations with a number of cities, taking control of much of the Iberian Peninsula.

In 228 BC, Hasdrubal the Fair founded the naval base and capital of New Carthage (perhaps old Mastia, now Cartagena). It was ideally situated near regional mines, while its natural harbour made interior lines of communications (including logistics and a communications network with Acra Leuce and Gadir) and trade with Carthage in North Africa much easier. The Carthaginian army, with which he accomplished the expansion of the Carthaginian footprint, now numbered 60,000 foot, 8,000 cavalry and 200 elephants. Its logistical train must have been enormous. The military strength and the new base demonstrated Carthage's regained wealth and status, rivalling that of Rome.

Another Roman mission was sent around 226/225 BC, but this one was to Hasdrubal the Fair at New Carthage at the time when Rome was

A coin from Iberia featuring a man's head on the obverse and and an armed horseman on the reverse.

battling Illyrian pirates in the Adriatic. An agreement was reached, and perhaps approved by Carthage, guaranteeing Carthaginian expansion but limiting its drive northwards. The northern and western parts of Iberia had never been part of the Carthaginian empire. The Ebro River became the demarcation line separating Carthaginian and Roman interests. The choice of the Ebro instead of the more natural geographical boundary of the Pyrenees was most likely sought by Rome for the protection of its ally Massilia, whose Greek colonies of Emporion (Emporiae) and Rhodes were along the north-eastern Iberian shores north of the Ebro. This suggests that former Massiliote colonies such as Hemeroscopium and Alonis (near modern Valencia) were already under Punic control. The arrangement equally implied that Rome and its Massiliote ally would not expand southwards. The small Greco-Iberian town of Saguntum, 160km south of the Ebro in the plain of Valencia, was an established trading partner with the city of Massilia. Rome took Saguntum into *fidum* (trust) perhaps by 231 BC, but the treaty concluded in 226/225 BC should have implied that Rome would also not use Saguntum to hinder Carthage's expansion in the agreed-upon territories.

The agreement can be seen as an indication that neither Hamilcar nor his successor Hasdrubal the Fair sought a war with Rome – certainly not at the time – even though Rome was engaged in long campaigns against the ever-menacing Gauls and Illyrians. There is no evidence suggesting Hasdrubal the Fair colluded with the Gauls against Rome, making it even less likely that the Carthaginians planned for a war with Rome. None of the Carthaginian commanders in Spain had rebuilt the Punic navy to challenge Roman naval superiority – another possible indication that none desired war. Some argue that the lifelong hatred of Rome by the Barcids may suggest this was a ruse, and that they always intended to attack Rome by land, lulling the Romans into a false sense of security by neglecting the navy Rome thought necessary for an invasion of Italy.

Despite all the years of Carthaginian presence, Iberia remained a volatile place. Sporadic revolts in North Africa also required military interventions. Hasdrubal the Fair was killed in 221 BC by either an Iberian slave avenging his master or a Celt who held a personal grudge. Hasdrubal's murder set the stage for the rise of the greatest of all Carthaginian commanders, Hannibal.

CHRONOLOGY

All dates are BC.

900–800   Phoenician expansion into Iberia.

814   Traditional date for founding of Carthage.

753   Traditional date for founding of Rome.

600–500   Multiple Greco-Carthaginian wars in Sicily, Sardinia and the Western Mediterranean. Carthage keeps Greeks out of Gadir, Iberia and most of the south-east of the peninsula. Ongoing warfare for control of Sicily.

509   First treaty between Carthage and Rome, recognizing Punic control over Sardinia and Corsica.

348   Second treaty between Rome and Carthage reaffirms the first treaty.

306   Third treaty between Rome and Carthage; Rome promises to stay out of Sicily, and Carthage out of Italy.

280–275   Roman and Carthaginian wars with Pyrrhus of Epirus on the Italian mainland and Sicily.

264–241   First Punic War.

255   Battle of Tunis; commander of Punic forces Xanthippus defeats Roman commander Regulus.

247   Hannibal is born; Hamilcar is appointed commander of the Sicilian campaign.

241–238/237   The Truceless War.

238   Rome illegally annexes Sardinia and Corsica.

237   Gadir becomes a base for Hamilcar's expansion into south-eastern Iberia.

236   Carthaginian campaigns against Iberian chiefs Istolatius and Indortes.

231   Hamilcar founds city of Acra Leuce.

231   Rome sends envoys to Hamilcar revealing their intent to pay off reparations.

229–228   Rome battles Illyrian pirates.

228   Battle of Helike; Hamilcar is killed.

228/227   Hasdrubal the Fair is elected Carthaginian commander, and founds the naval base and capital at New Carthage.

226   The Ebro understanding or treaty is agreed between Carthage and Rome.

225–222   Rome defeats the Gauls; war will continue against the Gauls to 193.

221   Hasdrubal the Fair is assassinated. Hannibal is elected commander of Carthaginian forces in the Iberian Peninsula.

221/220   Hannibal launches a successful campaign against Althea, the capital of the Olcades, who have allied themselves with the Vaccaei and Carpetani against Carthaginian expansion.

220   Battle of the Tagus River – Hannibal is victorious over the Iberian tribes of the Carpetani, Vaccaei, Vettones and Olcades.

220/219   In late summer, Roman envoys warn Hannibal not to advance beyond the Ebro River.

Rome fights the Second Illyrian War against a revived Illyrian power under Demetrius.

219   Saguntum is besieged and captured by Hannibal.

218	May: Rome demands the arrest of Hannibal – Carthage refuses. Rome plans a two-pronged attack, one in Spain under Publius Cornelius Scipio (the elder Scipio), and another under Tiberius Sempronius Longus on Sicily in preparation for an invasion of North Africa.
	Outbreak of the Second Punic War.
	May/June: Hannibal marches north, subduing tribes, en route to Rome.
	Battle of Cissa near Tarraco – a Roman victory.
	Battle of Ticinus – a Carthaginian victory.
	Battle of Trebia – a Carthaginian victory.
217	Battle of Lake Trasimene – a Carthaginian victory.
	Battle of the Ebro River – a Roman victory.
216	Battle of Cannae – a Carthaginian victory.
215	Battle of Dertosa/Ibera – a Roman victory.
214–205	First Macedonian War pits Rome against Philip V of Macedon (loosely allied with Carthage post-Cannae).
214	Syracuse joins Carthage.
212	Rome recaptures Saguntum.

A Carthaginian gold coin with horse and palm tree, dated roughly 390–380 BC. (18253552, Münzkabinett der Staatlichen Museen, Berlin; photograph by Dirk Sonnenwald)

212/211	Rome takes Syracuse in the autumn; the mathematician and inventor Archimedes is killed.
211	Battle of the Upper Baetis (twin clashes at Castulo and Ilorca), death of Gnaeus and the elder Scipio – both Carthaginian victories.
209	Publius Cornelius Scipio Africanus (the younger Scipio), the son of the elder Scipio, captures New Carthage – a Roman victory.
	Tarentum in Italy falls to Rome.
208	Battle of Baecula – indecisive outcome, as Hasdrubal withdraws in good order.
207	Hasdrubal crosses the Alps, and is killed at the Battle of the Metaurus.
207	Hannibal is limited to operations in Bruttium (Calabria, southern Italy).
206	Battle of Ilipa – a Roman victory.
	Battle of Carteia – a Roman victory.
	Mutiny against Scipio at Sucro.
	Romans capture Gadir.
205	Mago Barca fails to recapture New Carthage.
	Mago begins a two-year campaign in Liguria.
	Hannibal has his deeds carved into an altar at the Temple of Juno Lacinia (near Crotone, Calabria).
204	Conclusion of the First Macedonian War.
	Scipio invades North Africa from Sicily.
	Masinissa joins Scipio.
203	The Burning of the Camps and Battle of the Great Plains – Romano-Numidian victories.

A dermoplasty reconstruction of 'The Young Man of Byrsa', based on a skeletal remain in the National Museum of Carthage, Tunisia. The youth was a Phoenician who lived approximately 2,500 years ago and provides some sense of the typical appearance of Carthaginian males in the period under discussion.

	Syphax is captured by Masinissa and Laelius.
	Hannibal and Mago are recalled by Carthage.
	Mago is defeated in Cisalpine Gaul, and dies of wounds en route with his army to join Hannibal in North Africa.
202	Battle of Zama – a Romano-Numidian victory over Carthage, ending the Second Punic War.
201	Peace treaty between Carthage and Rome.
200–196	Second Macedonian War.
196	Hannibal is elected as suffete of Carthage.
195	Masinissa raids Carthaginian territories.
	Hannibal leaves Carthage in a forced exile instigated by Rome.
192–188	Rome battles the Seleucid King Antiochus III; Hannibal accompanies the king, but does not hold command.
189–187	Hannibal is in Crete, then Armenia.
187–83	Hannibal takes refuge at the court of King Prusias of Bithynia; he commands a fleet in a local war against Eumenes II of Pergamum.
186	Scipio enters self-imposed exile.
183	Death of Scipio.
183/181	Hannibal commits suicide by poison aged 64, having been betrayed by his host King Prusias of Bithynia.
172–168	Third Macedonian War.
169–167	Third Illyrian War.
151	Carthage declares war on Masinissa.
149–146	Third Punic War, and annihilation of Carthage.
112–106	Rome defeats the Numidian Jugurtha, illegitimate grandson of Masinissa.
19	Roman emperor Augustus conquers northern Hispania, bringing the entire peninsula under the control of Rome.

OPPOSING COMMANDERS

CARTHAGINIAN

Hamilcar Barca (275–228 BC) was a Carthaginian landed aristocrat and commander of Punic forces from 247 BC until his death in 228 BC. He may have been raised in Barce in Cyrenaica, North Africa, and was perhaps a new member of the Carthaginian aristocracy. It is not unreasonable to assume that the Phoenicians who settled Carthage had intermixed with Greek/Sicilian, southern European and native peoples of North Africa in the melting pot that was the city and region. At 28, Hamilcar commanded the Punic forces in Sicily (247–241 BC). He waged a guerrilla war against the Romans, raided Italy and negotiated a peace treaty on behalf of Carthage. Hamilcar commanded the Punic forces during the Truceless War (241–238/237 BC) in North Africa. He became commander of the Punic forces in Spain in 237 BC until his death nine years later. He reinvigorated the Carthaginian presence in Spain and founded a new base called Acra Leuce (perhaps modern Alicante). Hamilcar Barca died in 228 BC either in a clash of arms or by drowning while misdirecting pursuers away from his sons while campaigning against the Vettones.

A bust of the Carthaginian general Hasdrubal the Fair, erected in Cartagena, Spain.

Hamilcar had three daughters and three sons. One daughter married Bomilcar, a Carthaginian *šūfeṭ* (a non-royal magistrate), who was possibly a naval commander during the Second Punic War. His grandson was Hanno, a nephew of Hannibal's, who served with the latter as a commander throughout the war. A second daughter married Hasdrubal the Fair (270–221 BC) making him Hamilcar's son-in-law. The last daughter married the Berber ally Naravas, who sided with the rebelling mercenaries during the Truceless War, but then switched allegiance to Carthage. Hannibal (247–183/181 BC) was the eldest son and the sole survivor of the three brothers during the Second Punic War. He died by his own hand around the age of 65. Hasdrubal (245–207 BC) was killed at the Battle of the Metaurus (207 BC) at the age of 38, and Mago (243–203 BC) probably died of wounds aged 40 en route to North Africa.

Hasdrubal the Fair (270–221 BC) was the son-in-law of Hamilcar and brother-in-law of Hannibal. He commanded

A statue of Hannibal Barca, erected in Cartagena, Spain.

forces sent to North Africa to quell a Numidian rebellion in 236 BC. He led Carthage in Spain after Hamilcar's death, crushing the Oretani, then used diplomacy to unify Carthaginian hegemony. In 227 BC, he founded a new naval base called New Carthage (Carthago Nova, modern Cartagena). Under Hasdrubal the Fair, Carthage and Rome came to an agreement in 226 BC defining Carthaginian hegemony up to the Ebro River while limiting Roman interests north of it. That same year, seven years after Hamilcar's death, Hasdrubal the Fair was assassinated in New Carthage.

Hannibal Barca (247–183/181 BC) commanded the Punic military after the death of Hasdrubal the Fair. He consolidated Punic hegemony in south-central and eastern Spain and launched a deep raid into north-west Spain. He fought his first successful open battle at the Tagus River (220 BC), showcasing his military genius. Hannibal conducted several sieges, notably at Saguntum in 219 BC (claimed by Rome as the *casus belli* for the Second Punic War), where he was wounded.

Hannibal departed Spain with 90,000 infantry, 12,000 cavalry and 37 elephants; he arrived in Italy with only 24,000 men and all the elephants. He waged a 16-year-long war against Rome, scoring numerous exceptional victories until the balance of power shifted and he was recalled to Carthage in 203 BC. Hannibal lost his final battle with an inferior army at Zama in 202 BC. He devoted himself to politics until 196 BC.

After being exiled from Carthage in 195 BC, having been falsely accused by Rome of colluding with Antiochus III of the Seleucids, Hannibal fled and travelled the eastern Mediterranean, from Tyre to Antioch and Ephesus (both in Turkey), Crete, Armenia and finally to Bithynia (Anatolia, Turkey). He became the naval commander of the Seleucid fleet and fought a losing naval engagement against the Romans and their allies during the Seleucid War (192–188 BC). Hannibal escaped to the court of Prusias of Bithynia, where he was betrayed when the king was pressured by Rome to surrender Hannibal. Hannibal Barca died either from an infection or by poison at his own hand, according to Livy: 'Then, cursing the person and the kingdom of Prusias and calling upon the gods of hospitality to bear witness to his breach of faith, he drained the cup. This was the end of the life of Hannibal.' His death occurred between 183 and 181 BC.

Hasdrubal Barca (245–207 BC) served as an officer in numerous Iberian campaigns waged by his father and his older brother Hannibal. In 218 BC, he became the commander of the Punic forces in Spain upon Hannibal's departure for Italy, at the head of 12,650 infantry, 2,550 cavalry and 21 elephants as well as a significant naval contingent. The size of the Punic forces was large enough to brush aside any native or Roman forces. Hasdrubal campaigned with mixed results in the Iberian Peninsula, which prevented him from reinforcing his older brother in 217 BC as planned. A Numidian revolt in 213/212 BC by Syphax, inspired and supported by Rome, led Hasdrubal to cross with an army to North Africa, where he defeated Syphax. Hasdrubal lost Saguntum to Roman forces, but later won the significant twin battles at the Upper Baetis (211 BC), in which both Scipio brothers were killed.

At Baecula in 208 BC, although beaten, Hasdrubal managed to retreat in good order, saving the majority of his army.

Later in 208 BC, Hasdrubal was again ordered to join Hannibal in Italy, as war was favouring the Romans throughout the Spanish and Italian theatres. The following year, 207 BC, Hasdrubal successfully crossed the Alps, having crossed the Pyrenees the previous year during winter, and invaded mainland Italy. He besieged Placentia without success, then marched towards his brother, only to be defeated and killed during the Battle of the Metaurus (his messengers had been intercepted and his planned route exposed). His severed head was thrown into Hannibal's encampment while African troops were paraded in chains before him. He was the first of the brothers to die, at the age of 38.

Mago Barca (243–203 BC) commanded Punic forces in Italy and Spain. Mago accompanied his father and brother in their Iberian campaigns before joining Hannibal's Italian army. He was considered an excellent cavalry commander. He fought at Trebia (218 BC), where he led an ambush force during a crucial part of the battle. Mago was the rear detachment commander during army movements across Italy. He fought alongside Hannibal and Celt-Iberian troops in the middle of the central battle line at the Battle of Cannae (216 BC). Mago served as a detachment commander in the Bruttium campaign, and eventually sailed to Carthage to present the rings of the fallen Roman knights and senators at Cannae. He was then tasked with raising an additional army to be sent to assist Hannibal, but instead only a fraction of its forces and finances – some 4,000 Numidian cavalry, 40 elephants and 500

A coin showing the head of Hasdrubal Barca.

talents – was sent to Locri, Italy. He became the commander of a new army comprising 12,000 infantry, 1,500 cavalry and 20 elephants (backed by 1,000 talents) destined to reinforce Hasdrubal's stuttering Iberian campaigns.

Sent to Spain once again, Mago continued to excel as a cavalry commander. He was instrumental at the twin battles of the Upper Baetis in 211 BC, where the elder Scipio attacked Mago, Masinissa and Indibilis along with Hasdrubal Gisco's army. The Carthaginians defeated and killed the elder Scipio near Castulo, then all three Carthaginian armies joined together and defeated Gnaeus at Ilorca. Mago continued to fight in Spain when Hasdrubal left for Italy, before eventually being forced to retreat to Gadir where he joined the more senior general Hasdrubal, son of Gisco. He suffered defeat at the Battle of Ilipa in 206 BC, but then launched several unsuccessful attacks including an attempt to recapture New Carthage, before fleeing with the remnants of his army to the Balearic island of Menorca (where the eastern port of Mahón is named after him).

In 205 BC, Mago, with 15,000 men and 30 quinqueremes, captured Genoa, and held northern Italy for nearly three years tying up seven Roman legions without fighting a major battle. However, his army was prevented from joining Hannibal in the south of the Italian peninsula. The following year, he received 6,000 foot and some cavalry reinforcements from Carthage (according to Livy, 7,000 troops, seven elephants and 25 warships). The Battle of Insubria in 203 BC was indecisive, although Mago (who may have been wounded) surrendered the field of battle. A victory might have changed the course of the war.

Mago was recalled to Carthage after the younger Scipio destroyed the armies of Hasdrubal, son of Gisco, and Hanno, son of Bomilcar, and Rome captured Syphax. While en route with his army in 202 BC to Carthage, Mago died of wounds. An alternative account by Roman biographer Cornelius Nepos (110–25 BC) states that Mago survived the war and remained with Hannibal until the Carthaginians ordered Mago's arrest in 193 BC, whereupon he escaped but then died either in a shipwreck or killed by slaves.

Numidian

Masinissa (*c*.238–143 BC) was a Numidian prince of the Massylii. Raised in Carthage, he subsequently fought against the Romans in Italy, notably at Cannae, and in Spain. He fought alongside the Carthaginians in the Iberian Peninsula from 211 BC until 206 BC, and proved to be an excellent cavalry commander. Masinissa's nephew Massiva had been captured after the Battle of Baecula in 208 BC, but was released by Scipio, even though Masinissa had played a part in the death of Scipio's father and uncle at the Upper Baetis. Masinissa subsequently switched to support the Romans, and was instrumental in defeating Carthage in North Africa, notably at the Battle of Zama, where his timely assault against Hannibal's rear lines swung victory in Rome's favour. He ruled as king and an ally of Rome from 201 BC until his death at the age of 90. During his reign, he encroached on Carthaginian territory, eventually leading to a Roman intervention and the destruction of Carthage two years after his death. Numidia was eventually annexed by Rome in 46 BC.

A coin probably depicting Masinissa wearing a diadem on the obverse. The reverse shows a horse rearing with a palm frond in the background. (CC BY-SA 2.5, Classical Numismatic Group, Inc. http://www.cngcoins.com)

Naravas was a Numidian of high rank. He fought with the mercenaries against Carthage during the Truceless War, before joining Hamilcar in 239 BC with 2,000 horsemen, tipping the scales in Carthage's favour. He married Hamilcar's third daughter.

Iberian

Indibilis and Mandonius were two kings of the Iberian Ilergetae, and were allied with Carthage. They fought in numerous battles against the Romans, and were often in revolt. The brothers subsequently switched allegiance to Rome in 209 BC, but fought against Rome again during the Roman mutiny against Scipio at Sucro, eastern Spain, in 206 BC. Though defeated, they raised another large army, but were defeated once again; Indibilis was killed, and his brother Mandonius escaped with the remnants of their army.

A bust of the elder Scipio, father of Publius Cornelius Scipio Africanus, erected in Cartagena, Spain.

ROMAN

Publius Cornelius Scipio (d. 211 BC – the elder Scipio) was a Roman general and consul in Spain and Italy from 217 to 211 BC. He was the father of Publius Cornelius Scipio Africanus (the younger). The elder Scipio was too late to stop Hannibal crossing the Rhone in September 218 BC, and sent his brother Gnaeus Cornelius Scipio Calvus along with his consular army to Spain while he returned to Italy hoping to intercept Hannibal. He lost the Battle of Ticinus in 218 BC, where he was wounded. The elder Scipio and Tiberius Sempronius Longus were defeated at the Battle of Trebia. He then went to Iberia, where his brother had secured northern Spain, north of the Ebro. He defeated Hasdrubal's army in 215 BC at Dertosa, putting an end to Carthaginian ambitions of reinforcing Hannibal by land. The brothers captured Saguntum in 212 BC. The elder Scipio was killed in 211 BC near Castulo at the Battle of the Upper Baetis.

Gnaeus Cornelius Scipio Calvus (d. 211 BC) was the older brother of the elder Scipio and a commander of two Roman legions (V and VI) in Spain from 217 BC until

A Roman denarius depicting on the obverse the younger Scipio, with a trident at left. On the reverse, Jupiter stands between the goddesses Juno and Pallas; below them is the word 'ROMA' with an eagle.

his death. He arrived with his brother's consular army in northern Spain, where he secured a Roman foothold north of the Ebro River by defeating a Carthaginian fleet and raiding New Carthage and Ebusus (Ibiza). He waged several successful campaigns against Carthage and prevented Hasdrubal from reinforcing his brother in Italy. In 211 BC, Gnaeus was defeated and killed within a month of his younger brother's death during the twin battles of the Upper Baetis, near Ilorca.

Publius Cornelius Scipio Africanus (236–184/183 BC – the younger Scipio), at the age of 25, took command of the reconstituted consular army in Spain, composed of survivors and garrison troops and the remnants of disbanded Campanian legions. He then began to subdue Spain, never losing a set battle. For his victory over Hannibal and Carthage, he was awarded the surname 'Africanus'. He participated in the Battle of Ticinus, where his father was wounded but was saved by him and his best friend Gaius Laelius. He captured New Carthage in a daring surprise twin attack from land and sea. The younger Scipio was victorious at Baecula in 208 BC and Ilipa in 206 BC. After securing Spain, he spent time training his army in Sicily, and went on to defeat three armies in North Africa, including Hannibal's at Zama in 202 BC.

In later years in Rome, the younger Scipio was frequently attacked by politicians when he opposed Rome's desire for revenge against Hannibal. He withdrew from public life to a farm where, embittered and ill, he died in 184 or 183 BC.

Gaius Laelius (c.235–c.160 BC) was the younger Scipio's closest friend and comrade in arms, who helped save the life of the latter's father at the Battle of Ticinus. He commanded the Roman fleet during the assault on New Carthage and carried the news of the tremendous victory to Rome. During the battle at Baecula, Laelius led the left wing of the consular army in a tactical movement atypical of the traditional Roman order of battle. Laelius raided the Libyan coast, while the younger Scipio's army was being trained in Sicily for the invasion of North Africa. During his raid, he met with Masinissa, who had lost a civil war to Carthage's Numidian ally, and sealed the bond that led to Masinissa's alliance with Rome, and to Carthage's ultimate demise. He commanded the cavalry at the decisive Battle of Zama. After the war, Laelius advanced from aedile in 197 BC to praetor the next year and to consul in 190 BC, when he was the colleague of the younger Scipio's brother. In 167 BC, he befriended the Greek historian Polybius, whom he supplied with a great deal of information about the life of the younger Scipio.

OPPOSING FORCES

Carthage was renowned for its agriculture and trade. The natural harbour of the Punic capital was developed for both commercial and military operations. The wealth of the city afforded it vast defensive systems encircling it, large military and mercantile fleets and, crucially, mercenaries. Carthage subjugated neighbouring territories, but, unlike Rome, the peoples it conquered did not always enjoy the rights of citizenship or the special privileges that Rome extended to the defeated. Carthage's relations with North African native peoples was complicated and at times ruthless, especially during phases of rebellion. Some native peoples switched sides repeatedly during the Punic Wars. Alliances were shored up with marriages of Numidian and Iberian royalty.

The city of Rome may have numbered 90,000 people in our period. In a 265 BC census, Republican Roman male citizens aged 17 and older numbered 292,234, while Latins and other allies provided 550,000 men. The total population of the republic reached approximately 3 million people along with slaves. According to Greek historian and geographer Strabo (64/63 BC to c.AD 24), Carthage had 700,000 residents – yet that number is disputed by

LEFT
An example of a bronze disc breastplate common during the Punic Wars. This one is held at National Archaeological Museum in Madrid and is dated between 500–376 BC. (Michelle Ricci)

FAR LEFT
A limestone example from the 1st century BC to perhaps later of a northern Celt-Iberian horseman. Note the small round shield similar to the *caetra*. He seems to be wearing some kind of helmet. Other shields are barely visible, perhaps indicating his many victories over his enemies. Held in the National Archaeological Museum in Madrid. (Michelle Ricci)

modern archaeological estimates of 100,000–200,000 with approximately 2 million people under its rule throughout its North African hegemony. Other estimates range from 90,000 up to 800,000. Whatever the correct figure, in general terms both warring cities encompassed large populations.

Rome, Latin and Allies (based on paper strength per legion)

Year (BC)	Legions	Romans	Allies	Total
218	6	26,000	44,000	70,000
217	11	50,000	75,000	125,000
216	15	75,000	100,000	175,000
215	15	50,000	50,000	100,000
214	20	75,000	75,000	150,000
213	22	75,000	75,000	150,000
212	25	80,000	80,000	160,000
211	25	80,000	80,000	160,000
210	21	65,000	65,000	130,000
209	21	65,000	65,000	130,000
208	21	60,000	60,000	120,000
207	23	70,000	70,000	140,000
206	20	60,000	60,000	120,000
205	18	50,000	50,000	100,000
204	19	55,000	55,000	110,000
203	20	60,000	60,000	120,000
202	16	50,000	50,000	100,000

Table reproduced with permission from Michael James Taylor, *Finance, Manpower, and the Rise of Rome*, PhD dissertation, University of California, Berkeley, 2015

During the Second Punic War, Carthage's revenues and manpower mobilization equalled (and at times exceeded) that of Rome. Nonetheless, Rome's republican system of government, its expansive system of citizenship and its exploitation of Italian subjects for military service allowed it to raise unusually large military forces despite a limited fiscal base. Troop strengths listed in ancient sources are often disputed. In 225 BC, as Rome struggled with a major Gallic war, Polybius lists in detail the Roman and allied forces available: two consuls with four legions each fielded 5,200 infantry and 300 cavalry, while allies supplied 30,000 foot and 2,000 cavalry. Sabines and Etruscans totalled 50,000 infantry and 4,000 horsemen. Umbrians and Sarsinatae (hill tribes of the Apennine district) provided 20,000, with the same number provided by the Veneti and Genomani. Roman reserves comprised 20,000 infantry and 3,000 citizen cavalry, with allies providing another 30,000 foot and 2,000 mounted. Also available for service were 80,000 foot and 5,000 cavalry from the Latins; Samnite forces totalling 70,000 foot and 7,000 cavalry; 50,000 foot and 16,000 horse from the Iapygians and Messapians; 30,000 foot and 3,000 cavalry from the Lucanians; and 20,000 foot and 4,000 cavalry offered by the Marsi, Marrucini, Frentani and Vestini. On Sicily and at Tarentum were two reserve legions, each comprising 4,200 foot, and 2,000 horse. Romans and Campanians provided 250,000 foot and 23,000 horse. The forces defending Rome were over 150,000 infantry and 6,000 cavalry. The total manpower was in excess of 700,000 foot and 70,000 horse (Livy cites 300,000 total). Polybius notes that Hannibal, upon his arrival in Italy, had fewer than 20,000 troops to oppose this immense force.

Comparative strengths during the Second Punic War

Carthage and Allies

Year	218 BC	218/217 BC	215/214 BC	204 BC	203 BC	202 BC
Spain	26,000	26,000	60,000			
Gaul (Transalpine and Cisalpine)	59,000			20,800	20,800	
Sardinia			19,000			
Italy		40,000	67,000	15,000	15,000	
Africa	19,000	19,000	19,000	93,000	30,000	50,000
Total manpower	104,000	85,000	165,000	128,800	65,000	50,000
Roman legions						
Number of legions	6	6	15	19	20	16
Total manpower	70,000	70,000	100,000	110,000	150,000	100,000
Carthagian strength as percentage of Roman strength	**150 per cent**	**120 per cent**	**165 per cent**	**115 per cent**	**45 per cent**	**50 per cent**

Table reproduced with permission from Michael James Taylor, *Finance, Manpower, and the Rise of Rome*, PhD dissertation, University of California, Berkeley, 2015

Rome enjoyed naval superiority during the Second Punic War, even though both sides built hundreds of warships throughout the war. In Spain, the superiority of the Roman crew was due to the number of seamen drawn from Greek colonies, such as Massilia. A few sea battles were fought, notably at the Ebro in 217 BC, but throughout the Iberian campaign Carthage never challenged Roman naval superiority. The use of the Roman fleet was evident throughout the campaigns, notably during the capture of New Carthage in 209 BC. The Punic fleet on occasion managed to reinforce the campaigns in Iberia and in Italy. It also aided Hasdrubal, son of Gisco, and Mago Barca to escape to Gadir and then on to Carthage and Italy respectively.

CARTHAGINIAN

Very little is known about the Carthaginian army. We do know that in the centuries preceding the Punic Wars, Carthage fielded a Greek-style phalanx of citizens called the Sacred Band of Carthage; its 2,500 men were supposedly trained from an early age and represented the elite of Carthage's youth. It formed a reserve force for its regular citizen army, which may have numbered 7,500 in strength. We may assume that its fighting technique was based on the predominant Greek phalanxes, using spears and round shields. During the Greco-Punic Wars (580–265 BC) fought for control of Sicily, the Sacred Band was destroyed at the Battle of the Crimissus in 339 BC on the island. Thereafter, and unable to sustain citizen losses, Carthaginian forces became primarily defensively oriented, supplementing their armies with Libyans, Liby-Phoenicians and a multitude of mercenaries who bore the brunt of battle. To the best of our knowledge, all the Punic armies were officered by Carthaginian citizens.

The armies of Carthage included (but were not limited to) Liby-Phoenicians; Libyans; Lergetae (perhaps an unknown African tribe and not Spanish); Numidians (lumped into Berbers) of the Massylian,

Composition of the Punic-Iberian army

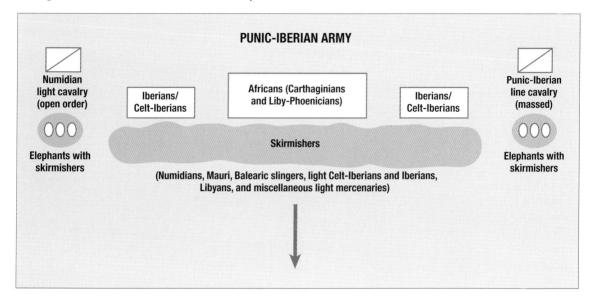

PUNIC-IBERIAN ARMY

Numidian light cavalry (open order)

Elephants with skirmishers

Iberians/ Celt-Iberians

Africans (Carthaginians and Liby-Phoenicians)

Iberians/ Celt-Iberians

Punic-Iberian line cavalry (massed)

Elephants with skirmishers

Skirmishers

(Numidians, Mauri, Balearic slingers, light Celt-Iberians and Iberians, Libyans, and miscellaneous light mercenaries)

Masaesylian and Maccoeian tribes; Maurian tribes; Balearic islanders; Iberians; Celt-Iberians; Celts; Greeks; and even Roman deserters.

Liby-Phoenicians or Africans

We are hampered by the lack of evidence or surviving texts to conclusively state who made up the African troops. North Africa featured a complex tapestry of nomadic and semi-nomadic peoples as well as various ethnicities, and other northern and eastern peoples invading or settling along the shores of the continent bordering the Mediterranean.

Hasdrubal's ethnicity may have included Greek ancestry and we cannot discount some African heritage to whatever degree. We assume the Liby-Phoenicians were a mix of Phoenician Carthaginians and Libyan Berbers, racially and culturally intermixed. However, we also know that in the 6th century BC, Carthaginian residents already included genetic markers from either Spain or the islands in the Mediterranean.

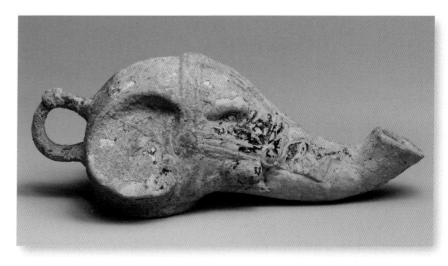

A terracotta lamp in the form of an elephant's head, a Greco-Sicilian find dating to the 3rd century BC. Alexander the Great brought Greek culture into contact with animals from India and the elephant became a popular representation on Hellenistic coins. With the Carthaginian influence on Sicily during the Punic Wars, elephants, usually depicted as war animals, also became common in Sicilian art. (The Met Museum)

Other Berber tribes included the Numidians, the Masaesyli, the Massylii and the Mauri (Moors). To the west and to the south of the Numidians and Moors lived the Gaetulians. The Libyans were a subject Berber people but provided a solid core to the Carthaginian army. We assume that the African troops were armed similarly to the Greeks (perhaps with linen armour, round shields and spears as a primary weapon) and fought in phalanxes. Perhaps some accommodations were made in their armour for the environmental conditions of North Africa, since at that time this area was lusher and greener than the northern regions of the Mediterranean.

A well-preserved example of a falcata, a popular type of sword in the Iberian Peninsula from the 5th to the 1st century BC. Its blade is double-edged for about half of its length. The wood grip is a modern addition.

The Mauri
The Mauri were Berber mercenaries, and may have been used as archers and skirmishers. They were perhaps lightly armed with javelins or spears, and equipped with round shields. In all likelihood, they operated alongside Balearian slingers, screening the main army and occupying difficult terrain.

The Balearians
These highly sought-after islanders were famous slingers capable of accurate and deadly fire with their stone and metal projectiles. For different ranges, the slingers used a variety of slings. They may have used small shields to parry incoming missile attacks. Their roles included opening battle skirmishes, harassing enemy skirmishers, covering river crossings and traversing challenging terrain.

A small bronze statue dated to the 2nd century BC found in Malaga. Note the similarity of the lion skin to representations of Hercules. More small bronze statues like this one have been found in the vicinity of the Strait of Gibraltar than anywhere else in Spain. (Michelle Ricci)

The Numidians
The Numidians are the best-known allies of Carthage and Rome during the Punic Wars. They provided arguably the finest light cavalry of their time. They were primarily used to harass or outflank the enemy on their sturdy, smaller horses, which were ridden bareback with only a single rein for control. The Numidians wore simple tunics, possibly sheepskin cloaks or other animal hides, and carried javelins, with some using small, light, round shields. As a nomadic or semi-nomadic people they were accustomed to the rigours of the outdoors and spending considerable time on horseback. They were excellent scouts. In combat, they could close on the enemy quickly, hurl a shower of javelins and then retreat, repeating these tactics until out of javelins. Interestingly, the light cavalry often defeated the more heavily equipped Roman cavalry. This may have been due to their greater numbers and the use of javelins.

A terracotta statue of Baal Hammon, the chief deity of Carthage, shown here seated on his throne, flanked by sphinxes, and wearing a crown. He was a weather god considered responsible for the fertility of vegetation, and was commonly depicted as a bearded, older man with curling ram's horns. (CC BY-SA 4.0)

The Numidians were fierce and courageous under proper leadership. Ancient sources speak of the fear their appearance spread throughout Roman ranks, even if the soldiers were behind palisades. Once the Numidians joined the Romans, Carthage lost one of its greatest and most needed combat arms.

Numidians also provided infantry, and some of them were trained by Romans during the Punic Wars, depending on which side they were on at the time. They suffered extreme casualties (as at Zama in 202 BC) and are often ignored by ancient writers. Sometimes the foot soldiers fought alongside their mounted comrades, and some also fought more akin to light and line infantry in formation (probably open order). The Romans had trained Syphax's men, and Masinissa's Numidians may also have received some training and equipment. We assume that the infantry had a variety of arms and perhaps armour to be able to withstand regular enemy infantry.

Iberian/Celt-Iberian Warriors

For our purposes, we shall include the Celt-Iberians along with the Iberians as both lived in the Spanish theatre of war, although Celt-Iberians are unique in their own right. The Celt-Iberians included the Vettones and Vaccaei, the Callaeci of the north-west, the Asturian-Cantabrians and the Celtici of the south-west. Throughout their history, Iberians were able to field large armies and offered pitched battles. Their dress was probably a kind of white linen with a purple border; Polybius informs us this was a type of national dress for the Iberians.

The Iberians provided cavalry and infantry to Carthage. Although at times maligned by ancient chroniclers for their apparent ill discipline and wildness, they were in fact hardened warriors and proved difficult to defeat for both Carthage and Rome. Shifting allegiances, sometimes purchased, or at other times because of perceived insults or disreputable behaviour by Carthaginians or Romans alike, caused rifts and often broke out into open rebellion. An easy people to subjugate they were not. The Iberians and Celt-Iberians provided core components to the Carthaginian commanders in Spain and in Italy, but also to the Romans throughout the campaigns. Some of them were shipped to Carthage, replacing African troops destined to fight in Spain and Italy. Iberian troops were crucial in holding the centre line, fighting alongside Hannibal and Mago, at the Battle of Cannae. In the Iberian campaigns they were described as inferior to the African troops, but that may very well be a Roman bias, as the consular army often saw their Spanish allies desert. The Carthaginians had similar experiences, including Hannibal on his march overland – yet the Spanish fighters continued to populate both armies, providing a tough fighting edge.

In general terms, the infantry in the Iberian campaigns should not be considered heavy. They mostly matched the *hastati* and perhaps the *principes* in armaments. Personal body armour was limited during the Iberian war. Most fought with little if any armour, instead wearing large leather belts, or small disks to protect their chests akin to the Roman *hastatus*'s *pectorale*, and many wore helmets probably made of sinew or a combination of leather with sinew (although some used metal helmets). Large shields were employed by some infantry, similar to those of the Celts and also to the Roman *scutum*; these fighters were called *scutarii*. Others (the *caetrati*) carried small round shields about 60cm in diameter. They used a variety of javelins and spears, including a version which some scholars believe the Roman *pilum* was based upon. However, their primary weapon was the falcata sword, which featured a very strong blade with a slight curve. This, too, was supposedly adapted and modified by the Romans into the *gladius* – they may have first encountered this during the First Punic War. Iberian forces were subdivided into *speirai*, similar to Roman maniples and capable of fighting Romans in pitched battles. In many ways, the Iberians were similar to the Romans in uniform and their ability to fight pitched battles. The differences, however, may very well have lain in a lack of unified command, organization, logistics and unity of purpose. The Iberians were formidable fighters in close or open order of battle, similar to the Roman legionaries.

ROMAN

Composition of the Roman consular army

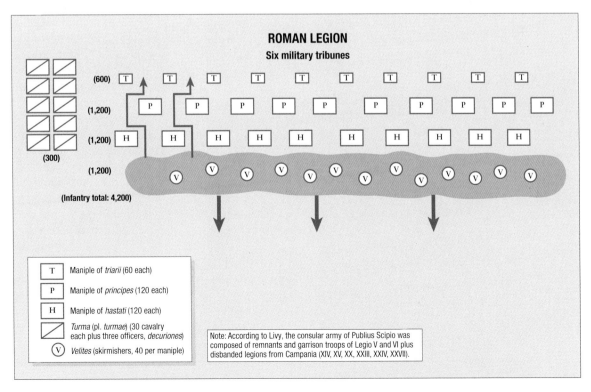

ROMAN LEGION
Six military tribunes

(600)
(1,200)
(1,200)
(300)
(1,200)
(Infantry total: 4,200)

T	Maniple of *triarii* (60 each)
P	Maniple of *principes* (120 each)
H	Maniple of *hastati* (120 each)
	Turma (pl. *turmae*) (30 cavalry each plus three officers, *decuriones*)
V	*Velites* (skirmishers, 40 per maniple)

Note: According to Livy, the consular army of Publius Scipio was composed of remnants and garrison troops of Legio V and VI plus disbanded legions from Campania (XIV, XV, XX, XXIII, XXIV, XXVII).

A bronze 6th-century BC helmet from Italy, of Picene origin. (The Met Museum)

An early 20th-century depiction of a Roman light-armed infantryman. His armour consists solely of an Etruscan-style helmet. Such helmets have been found in tombs as early as the 7th century BC, and have been found on the battlefield of Cannae (216 BC), indicating they were worn at the time of the Second Punic War. (Vinkhuizen Collection, New York Public Library)

The consular army was composed of four legions: two Roman and two drawn from allies. The Roman legion at the time was not a heavily armoured unit. The paper strength of each legion was 4,200 infantry and between 200 and 300 *equites* (knights on horseback). The infantry component was divided into four troop types. The youngest and most lightly armed skirmishers were the *velites*, used to initiate battles and to tackle the enemy's elephants. Sometimes, they would be used to pin forces down as the regular armed infantry executed tactical manoeuvres. *Velites* numbered 1,200 and were armed with javelins, sometimes brass helmets or animal skins, and carried round, lightweight shields; they acted as a screen for the entire legion.

The front rankers of the legion were the *hastati*, men with some experience. Their armour consisted of a palm-sized chest plate and some type of helmet, and they were armed with javelins (*pila*), short swords (*gladii*), and oblong, large shields (*scuta*). These soldiers should not be considered heavy infantry, and most likely were not all issued chest plates, which really only protected the heart. The next troop type, positioned behind the *hastati*, were the more experienced men who were also wealthier, and thus able to afford more substantial armour like chain mail: the *principes*. Some may still have worn chest plates. The men also fought with javelins and short swords, carried oval shields and wore helmets as the frontrankers did. Like the *hastati*, the *principes* numbered 1,200 men. The veteran campaigners formed the final line, the *triarii*. In terms of equipment, the only difference with the *principes* was the use of spears instead of javelins and that they were probably equipped with mail armour, being the most seasoned soldiers and possibly more wealthy. The

veterans, however, only numbered 600, giving a total of 4,200 legionaries. An allied legion was nearly identical, with the exception of the cavalry. Allied cavalry numbered between 600 and 900 horsemen. A consular army fielded 16,800 infantry and 1,600–2,400 cavalry. The tremendous contribution of Italian allies during the campaigns in Iberia and the war in general cannot be dismissed.

Organizationally, the legion was subdivided into smaller units called maniples (*manipulus* singular) and there were ten. Each *manipulus* was administratively divided into two equal-strength sub-units called *centuriae*. Each *centuria* held 60 men. The front was called the *centuria prior* and the rear the *centuria posterior*. In formation, each *manipulus* had a 20-man front and was six ranks deep, totalling 120 men.

The cavalry of 300 was divided into ten squadrons, or *turmae*. The *turmae* also had three officers called *decuriones* and three rearguard *optiones*. The allied cavalry would be similar in organization.

On the battlefield, the army was almost always anchored on either side by its cavalry. The infantry deployment in the field looked like a three-deep chequerboard, a triple *acies*, with skirmishers placed in front of them. The two Roman legions were in the centre of the battle line with one allied legion to its side. The Roman cavalry traditionally deployed on the right with the allied horse on the left wing. The *velites* screened the entire army, but at times were called to hold the centre, pinning enemy forces, while the maniples manoeuvred to the flanks for a pincer attack. The weakness of the legion was its lack of cavalry, which was useful for scouting, harassing and pursuing enemy forces. Another problem was its rigidity; the Iberian battlefields required tactical flexibility. It is an exaggeration to state that the legion was not composed of professionals.

ABOVE LEFT
An early 20th-century watercolour of a Roman cavalryman. He is unarmoured, and carries a spear and sword. (Vinkhuizen Collection, New York Public Library)

ABOVE RIGHT
An early 20th-century watercolour of a Capuan cavalryman, shown lightly armed without shield or armour. (Vinkhuizen Collection, New York Public Library)

OPPOSING PLANS

The overall Carthaginian strategic plan for the Second Punic War was based on Hannibal's plan to take his veteran army, secure his lines of communications as best as possible as he crossed the two mountain ranges of the Pyrenees and the Alps, and take the war directly to Rome's front door. He needed new Celtic allies to compensate for his anticipated losses during his trek. Carthaginian reinforcements were to come from Hasdrubal overland from Spain throughout the Second Punic War because Rome enjoyed uncontested naval superiority.

Once in Italy, Hannibal hoped to pin and defeat the Roman legions, thereby securing more allies while ripping the Roman confederacy apart, resulting in the reduction of Roman manpower. Once accomplished, the balance of power would shift to the great Carthaginian commander, forcing Rome into a peace treaty that guaranteed Carthage's survival and freedom from Roman ambition. The key was the arrival of follow-on forces led by his brother Hasdrubal. Hannibal departed with an army of 90,000 foot, 12,000 cavalry and 37 elephants, leaving behind enough troops to tackle any Roman incursion into northern Spain, thereby preventing Rome from gaining a foothold and leaving it unable to hinder Hasdrubal's march the following year (217 BC) to Italy. Hasdrubal's army was composed of 11,580 Africans, 300 Ligurians, 500 Balearic slingers, 2,550 cavalry and 21 elephants. He needed to raise more men for his future campaign; Iberia provided the money and the men for it.

Roman strategy for a war against Hannibal and Carthage was twofold. First, the army of the elder Scipio was to take on the Punic empire in Iberia by using Massilia as a base for operations into the Iberian Peninsula north of the Ebro River at Emporion, while simultaneously launching an attack against Carthage in North Africa. By 218 BC, the pro-consuls Scipio and Tiberius Sempronius Longus were in command of two consular armies, each comprising two legions. The two armies can be broken down as follows: Scipio's comprised 8,000 legionaries, 600 Roman *equites*, 14,000 allied infantry, 1,600 cavalry and 60 ships, for a total of 22,000 foot and 2,200 horse; Longus' army was of a similar composition, but with an additional 2,000 allied infantry, 200 cavalry and 160 quinqueremes (ships with five banks of oars), giving him 24,000 infantry and 2,400 cavalry.

Rome's naval supremacy since the First Punic War was ensured by a steady expansion of its number of ships. History had shown Carthage's vulnerability to invasions of North Africa. Although both the attempts by Agathocles of Syracuse (361–289 BC) and the Roman consul Marcus

Atilius Regulus (307–250 BC) resulted in defeats, they demonstrated a vulnerability that could be exploited. Crucial to a successful campaign were alliances with subject peoples of Carthage in North Africa, and Longus' mission there may very well have entailed securing new allies prior to launching an invasion, since two legions may not have been sufficient to capture Carthage.

The Carthaginians, however, could also consider history to be on their side, given their support for Rome during its battle for survival against Pyrrhus of Epirus, who had twice defeated Roman legions and nearly forced Rome into submission. Hannibal may very well have thought he, too, could force Rome to yield. Another strategic consideration was that some of Rome's allies had defected to Pyrrhus. How loyal the allies would remain should Hannibal defeat the Romans in battle was yet to be seen. Nonetheless, the historical record for both parties seemed promising, perhaps more so for Hannibal. What if he could find a secure base in Italy for his operations? During the First Punic War, Carthage did not seem to think it could locate a friendly area to operate from, but perhaps this time, coupled with military victories, Hannibal might emerge as the conqueror of Rome.

Another calculation was the continuous threat posed by the Celts in northern Italy. Any delay in the Carthaginian plan could allow Rome to crush them permanently and free itself to focus on Macedon and Carthage. The political situation seemed ripe for Hannibal to strike at Italy directly, and secure Celtic allies while defeating Roman consular armies in the field. The challenges, though, were numerous: the manpower and logistics required to traverse two mountain ranges through hostile territories; the need to secure more allies; pinning and defeating the highly vaunted Roman legions to foment rebellion of Rome's allies; and forcing their arch enemy into either submission or at least a peace that guaranteed Carthaginian hegemony and survival. In the meantime, Iberia needed to remain secure, as did Carthage itself.

As with all plans, when the first slingshot was launched they encountered significant friction. One of the key changes to the initial Carthaginian strategy was the arrival of the Roman consular army north of the Ebro, and its success in repulsing Hasdrubal's attacks. Having established a foothold, they now blocked the path to Italy through the mountain ranges.

Like Rome, Carthage was facing challenges nearer to home. Continuous rebellions by Numidian tribes required Hasdrubal's attention, as did the never-ending revolts in Iberia. Such fog of war impeded the primary mission to join Hannibal in Italy. Armies were chewed up in subjugating rebellions as well as replacing losses caused by Roman arms.

Hannibal's incredible victories in the early years of the war led to a change in Carthaginian strategy. No longer was the war to be fought in Italy.

This is an early 20th-century artist's impression of a Roman *eques*, or knight. His clothing appears expensive and he wears a form of body armour. (Vinkhuizen Collection, New York Public Library)

OPPOSITE
An Iberian bronze statuette of a warrior, dating from around the 5th century BC. The arrangement of the broad belt, short-sleeved tunic and pointed defensive garment covering the lower body is seen in Iberian art exclusively on warriors. This kind of costume is described by Strabo in his discussion of Iberian mercenary warriors and their dress. (The Met Museum)

Olive trees growing in Andalucia, Spain. During ancient times, Iberia had a vibrant agriculture, and its silver mines offered rich mineral resources.

Instead, alliances and reinforcements were to create a greater regional war, including Sicily and Macedon, with renewed efforts to supply Hannibal in Italy with men and money.

For Rome, the early disastrous defeats were temporary setbacks. It continued in its attempts to wrest control of Iberia's strategic assets, chiefly its silver mines and agricultural wealth, away from Carthage and to use them to fund its war efforts. As such, Rome continuously fielded armies and avoided major clashes in Italy against Hannibal. Iberia was the key. A victory in the peninsula would reverse fortune and boost Roman and allied morale. The stakes in Iberia were high for the overall conduct of the Second Punic War.

THE CAMPAIGN

221–220 BC: THE TAGUS

In 221 BC, Hannibal was elected commander of Punic-Iberian field forces by the army and subsequently ratified by Carthage. He was 25, at a time when the average life expectancy was between 35 and 40 years of age. Hannibal's first task was the submission of the Olcades, and he did so by besieging and capturing their city of Althea (Livy calls it Cartala) and imposing reparations on them. He retired to New Carthage for winter quarters, where he paid his victorious army well, thus ensuring their continued loyalty. Like many Carthaginians, Hannibal married locally: Himilce was an Iberian princess, and the daughter of King Murco of the Oretani from the city of Castulo.

By early 220 BC, Hannibal, in his second year of command, attacked Iberian tribes in north-western Spain. Accompanied in all likelihood by his excellent

A relief from Osuna depicting an Iberian warrior with large oval shield, leather/sinew helmet and falcata. He is wearing a short linen tunic, typical of Iberian warriors.

officers Maharbal, his nephew Hanno, son of Bomilcar, and his younger brothers Hasdrubal and Mago, Hannibal moved north towards the Ebro and the Sierra de Toledo in central Spain to raid the central-northern territories, notably of the Vaccaei. The campaign's intended purpose was a far-ranging strike to demonstrate the power of Carthage in the north and to intimidate the native tribes. For this campaign, Hannibal used 25,000 infantry out of the 60,000 available at the time, sufficient numbers to retain a smaller logistical footprint yet powerful enough for its purpose. His intention was not to subjugate the tribes (as had been done with the Oretani and Olcades) and to incorporate them into his army, for the Carpetani and Vaccaei, even in defeat, never provided troops for his forces (although we are told of Carpetani deserters from Hannibal's army).

Hannibal had two possible routes for his attack into the north. His army may have marched from New Carthage through the Oretani-controlled areas, then through the

Roman legionaries carrying scutum shields; they appear to be wearing mail, and are helmeted. The relief is from Estepa, Seville, Spain and dates to the 1st century BC; it is on display at the Archaeological Museum of Seville.

Carpetani region, near where Hannibal's army was to be ambushed on its return voyage, as his army made its way way to target the Vaccaei and their cities of Helmantica (Salamanca) and Arbucala (Toro, in Zamora province). Alternatively, the Punic-Iberian forces may have advanced on a westerly route. The latter would have avoided the Carpetani territory to the north altogether by traversing the eastern end of the Sierra Morena, crossing the land of the Oretani perhaps near Castulo, towards the west; once in the territories of the Vettones, he would have used the route north from Emerita (Mérida) to Helmantica, to the cities of the Vaccaei. His army would have battled hostile local tribes and crossed several rivers during its march upcountry. Ultimately, the campaign was a success. Hannibal defeated the Vettones and Vaccaei, both Celt-Iberian tribes in the Durius (Douro) River region, and captured the towns of Helmantica and Arbucala, the latter after a lengthy siege.

The Battle of the Tagus River, 220 BC

On his return march from the north-western region of Arbucala to New Carthage, Hannibal's army eventually used an ancient route travelling from the north-west to the south-east from Iplacea (Roman Complutum, now Alcala de Henares, near Madrid) to his base New Carthage on the south-eastern shore.

Hannibal's veteran army, encumbered by its hard-won treasures, had to cross the Tagus River close to Driebes, not far from the Carpetani oppidum (fortified settlement) of Caraca. Plutarch describes the Carpetani as 'a people beyond the river Tagonius [Tagus], and they do not dwell in cities or villages, but on a large and lofty hill containing caves and hollows in the cliffs which look towards the north'. Recent archaeological excavations in Driebes, on the Virgen de la Muela hill near the Tagus River, discovered a Carpetani fortified oppidum, which may have become the Roman city of Caraca.

It was during this phase of his march that Hannibal's army of 25,000 infantry, thousands of cavalry and 40 elephants was ambushed by a superior force of Carpetani, Olcades, Vaccaei and Vettones, numbering 100,000 Iberians and Celt-Iberians. The defeated Olcades, Vaccaei and Vettones, who had been bested by Hannibal the previous year, stirred up the Carpetani against the Carthaginians encumbered by the spoils of war, which also served as an incentive for the native forces to attack.

The battle was waged at the Tagus River between the towns of Driebes and Illana. There are slightly differing accounts by Polybius and Livy on the dispositions of forces and the conduct of the battle, including Hannibal's route of march, the location of his camp or camps (and it is unclear whether or not the palisade mentioned in the accounts existed), and also the locations of enemy troops fording the river. We can locate and recreate the battle with a high degree of certainty, however, given recent discoveries.

According to the ancient sources, the Tagus River itself formed the battlefield. Polybius writes: 'Hannibal, with admirable skill and caution, slowly retreated until he had put the Tagus between himself and the enemy; and thus giving battle at the crossing of the stream.' The key point is that Polybius states that Hannibal's army turned around and moved back the way it had come, placing the Tagus to his front, thus indicating he had already crossed the river. Not wanting to be overtaken on land by superior numbers, he decided to meet the enemy at the Tagus, forgoing a battle on the plains. A battle in the open with 100,000 native troops clashing with the much smaller Punic-Iberian army would have been a foregone conclusion. Using the river, Hannibal forced the enemy to cross piecemeal. He accomplished this by building a fortification, blocking certain fords and funnelling the enemy's advance, resulting in them being fewer in number at several points of the Tagus, thereby negating their numerical advantage. As the native forces crossed the river, Hannibal unleashed his cavalry, cutting them down while his elephants killed the enemy struggling onto the river's banks. Many of the enemy infantry were also swept away by the river's current amid the clashes with the Punic-Iberian cavalry. Polybius writes: 'At length Hannibal turned the tables on the enemy, and, recrossing the river, attacked and put to flight their whole army, to the number of more than a hundred thousand men.'

Livy's account matches that of Polybius in many ways, adding some details, but differing on the passage and location of the battle. Livy writes that Hannibal's army was thrown into some confusion when an attack north of the Tagus was made. Hannibal refused battle because his army was in disarray following the attack, and the sheer size of the opposing force made an open battle undesirable. Moreover, his army would have its back to the river, making an escape problematic if not impossible without major casualties. Instead, Hannibal built a camp on the northern bank of the Tagus, then surreptitiously crossed the river once the enemy had settled down for the night. According to Livy, the next day:

> [Hannibal's] entrenchments had been carried just far enough to allow room for the enemy to cross over, and he decided to attack them during their passage of the river. The Carpetani together with the contingents of the Olcades and Vaccaei numbered altogether 100,000 men, an irresistible force had they been fighting on level ground. Their innate fearlessness, the confidence inspired by their numbers, their belief that the enemy's retreat was due to fear, all made them look on victory as certain, and the river as the only obstacle to it. Without any word of command having been given, they raised a universal shout and plunged, each man straight in front of him, into the river.

It is at this point that Hannibal's cavalry, a huge force according to Livy, emerged and clashed midstream; large portions of the native troops were swept away, while any survivors reaching the banks were trampled to death by the elephants. As the enemy retreated and tried to reorganize itself, Livy tells us that Hannibal threw in his well-organized infantry and crossed the river, driving the enemy from the northern bank. The Carthaginians then spent a few days laying waste to the region, and made the Carpetani submit.

BATTLE OF THE TAGUS RIVER, 220 BC (PP. 36–37)

At the Tagus, Hannibal's army of 25,000 foot, thousands of cavalry and 40 elephants was ambushed by a superior force of Carpetani, Olcades, Vaccaei and Vettones numbering 100,000 Iberians and Celt-Iberians. The Punic army was making its way back from its successful campaign against the Vettones and Vaccaei, having sacked the towns of Helmantica and Arbucala. Hannibal's treasure-laden army needed to cross the Tagus on its way to the home base of New Carthage.

The beginning of the battle, shown here, sees a growing number of ferocious Carpetani and allies rushing into battle to get at the Carthaginian army across the Tagus River (**1**). The river is flowing to the west with a current of 1m/sec and depths of up to 1.5m. The distance between the banks is about 40m. The Celt-

Iberians and Iberians are struggling in the water (**2**). Many native fighters are also being dragged away and drowned by the swift current (**3**). Hannibal is using a strategically placed palisade to funnel the enemy into disadvantageous places to ford (**4**). There are perhaps only three fords made available to them, where all the fighters are experiencing the same difficulties. Within the palisade, Hannibal hides a number of elephants accompanied by skirmishers and large numbers of cavalry. The first elephants are seen emerging from the camp, supported by skirmishers, ready to attack the struggling survivors making it onto the bank (**5**). Numidian and Iberian light cavalry use their height advantage to deadly effect, killing and stopping the assault in the river (**6**).

The victory was tremendous, and was Hannibal's first major one over an Iberian tribe in open battle. Its strategic value was not lost on Livy, although with some exaggeration: 'There was no part of the country beyond the Ebro which did not now belong to the Carthaginians, with the exception of Saguntum.'

Did Hannibal, as Livy suggests, build a camp first before crossing the river at night? Doing so would create an opportunity for the opposing forces to send troops over the river first, thereby surrounding Hannibal's army as it was busy fortifying its position. There seems no doubt that the Carpetani and allies lacked a proper command and control structure, for we are told by Livy that in the subsequent battle, they charged without orders and in disorder into the Tagus. Perhaps there was no single overall commander for the native tribes, who could

A limestone relief of an Iberian horseman found at Osuna, held at the National Archaeological Museum, Madrid, Spain. He wears a short tunic and wields a short, straight sword.

have coordinated an assault. A reasonable argument can be made that Hannibal indeed crossed the Tagus, pursued by some of the enemy's forces, who threw Hannibal's rearguard into disarray. The Carthaginian army surely could have crossed the river even while in contact with enemy forces, as long as the attack was not in overwhelming force. The Punic-Iberian army was safeguarded by cavalry and light infantry, while the enemy attacked in limited numbers, as their main army was slowly massing. It is likely that skirmishing may have caused some confusion among Hannibal's rearguard, while the main army crossed the obstacle with elephants, which either kept the enemy at bay or aided the Carthaginians by blocking the river's current with their large bodies as the men and mules crossed. A massed onslaught of all 100,000 may not have been possible, given the terrain and location of the various tribes. Certainly, a hefty skirmish seems feasible.

Recent archaeological research confirms the existence of a quadrangular structure that could correspond with a palisade built by Hannibal's men, but this was on the other (southern) side of the river. In front of the palisade was a furrow that seemingly served as a front-line trench similar to that of Roman marching forts. A small hill called El Jardín, located to the south-east of the palisade, overlooked the battle and could have served as a command post for Hannibal and his staff. The placement of the quadrangular palisade forced the enemy into crossing at strategic locations, negating their numerical superiority, reducing the width of their frontages and funnelling them into unfavourable positions.

We can paint a reasonable picture that Hannibal's army was marching south-east near the Carpetani fortified settlement, perhaps even beginning to cross the Tagus. It is likely his army had forward elements scouting ahead, and a rearguard protecting his main column. The flanks were no doubt covered by light cavalry. He threw advance reconnaissance elements forward, scouting for fords to cross, as his rearguard either noticed enemy

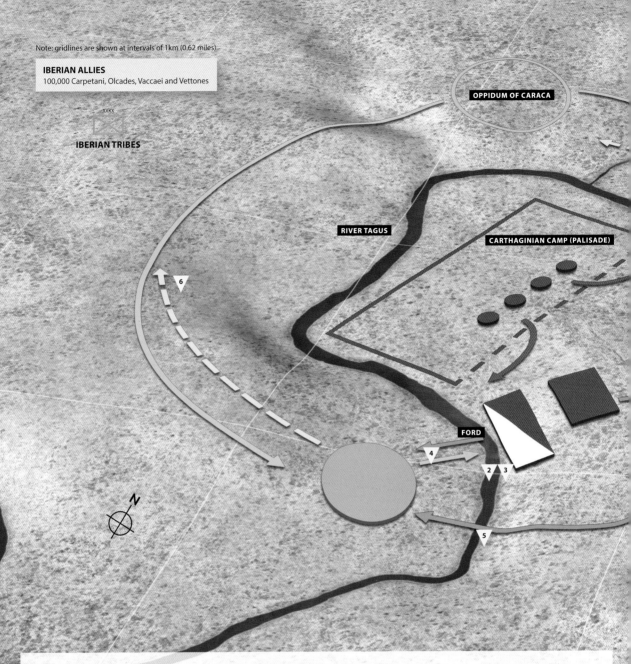

Note: gridlines are shown at intervals of 1km (0.62 miles)

IBERIAN ALLIES
100,000 Carpetani, Olcades, Vaccaei and Vettones

xxxx

IBERIAN TRIBES

OPPIDUM OF CARACA

RIVER TAGUS

CARTHAGINIAN CAMP (PALISADE)

FORD

6

4

2 3

5

N

BATTLE OF THE TAGUS RIVER, 220 BC

On his return march from Arbucala to New Carthage, Hannibal's army – encumbered by treasure – had to cross the Tagus River near the Carpetani oppidum of Caraca. Here, it was ambushed by a superior force of Carpetani, Olcades, Vaccaei and Vettones, but Hannibal used his cavalry and elephants to throw the attackers into disarray.

EVENTS

Phase 1

1. Having crossed the Tagus River with the main army, Hannibal receives reports of the growing number of the enemy Carpetani and allies. Alarmed by their numbers, he turns his force back towards the Tagus, where a palisade is erected.

2. The Carpetani and allies, having taken some time to organize themselves, cross the Tagus at fording points in pursuit of the Carthaginians.

Phase 2

3. Hannibal unleashes a large number of cavalry quickly against the Carpetani and allies as they are mid-stream crossing the Tagus. Men on foot struggle in the 1.5m-deep water and the current, being swept away, while simultaneously Punic-

Iberian cavalry decimate their ranks in the waters. The cavalry and elephants provide the hammer blows against the crossing-point anvils.

Phase 3

4. Thrown into panic and disarray, the leading Carpetani, Olcades, Vaccaei and Vettones retreat and collide with the mass of forward-moving men behind them.

5. Hannibal, aware of the situation, crosses the river with his infantry, probably at the extreme ends of his palisade, to support the cavalry. This pincer attack stops the Carpetani from reorganizing.

6. The Carpetani, Olcades, Vaccaei and Vettones flee, pursued by the Carthaginians.

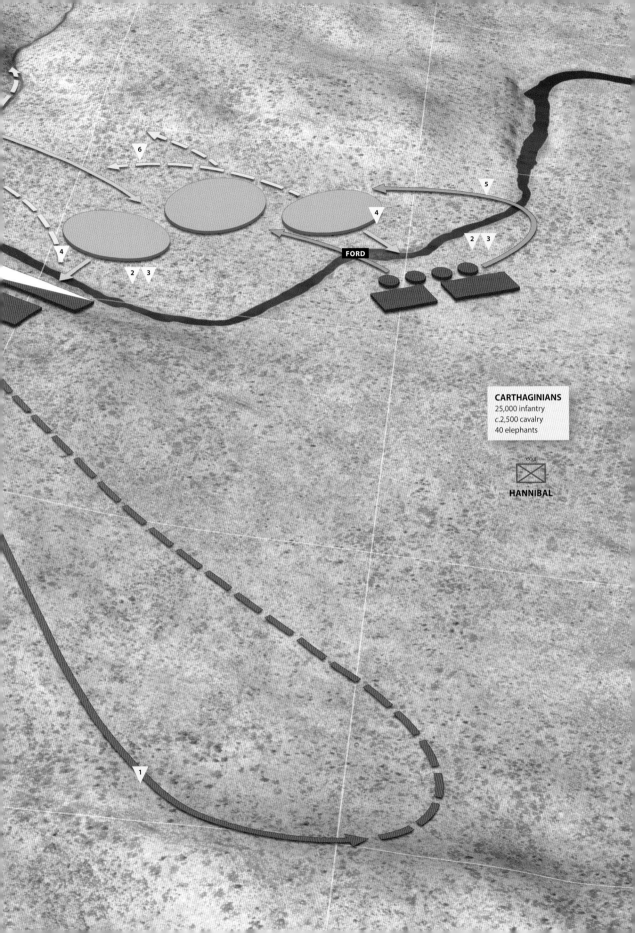

FORD

CARTHAGINIANS
25,000 infantry
c.2,500 cavalry
40 elephants

xxxx
HANNIBAL

movement or was perhaps already engaged in skirmish, thus explaining why Hannibal's army was thrown into disorganization.

The challenge for the native leaders at this point was the disposition of their large numbers. The logistical requirements must have placed a strain on the Carpetani. Most likely, the fighters were spread out over a large area and would have taken some time to assemble and to consolidate into their respective fighting units. Perhaps only small numbers attacked the Carthaginian column, causing confusion, but were unable to overrun it. Then, having crossed the river with the main army, Hannibal probably received reports of the growing number of the enemy and, alarmed by their size, turned his force back to the recently crossed Tagus, where he built a palisade. Aware of the places where his army had previously forded the river, he built the fortifications to force the enemy to cross at the most disadvantageous fords. If he had marched on, laden with loot and in pursuit, the Carpetani and allies would surely have caught his men in open terrain, and using their numerical superiority would have allowed the native people to extend their lines well beyond that of Hannibal's army. This would have been disastrous and likely would have resulted in an emphatic native victory. Turning back towards the river, building a palisade and forcing the enemy to split into smaller groups gave Hannibal a tactical advantage. The small hill to the south-east of the palisade provided him with an ideal command post to direct his troops. The palisade no doubt protected and hid Punic-Iberian troops and elephants, as we know that Hannibal unleashed a large number of cavalry quickly when the enemy was mid-stream. Had the Carpetani and allied forces been aware of the disposition of the Punic forces, they would not have crossed a deep, fast-moving river in the face of cavalry – unless of course, as Livy states, the enemy threw themselves without orders into the attack. Men on foot struggled in the deep water and many were swept away, while simultaneously Punic-Iberian cavalry decimated their ranks midstream. The cavalry and elephants were the hammer used at the crossing points. Assuming there were three crossing points, based on recent discoveries, that would mean three groups of a dozen or so elephants supported by light infantry patrolled the banks of the fords. Once the attacks were neutralized and thrown into panic, the Carpetani, Olcades, Vaccaei and Vettones retreated and collided with the mass of forward-moving men behind them. Hannibal, aware of the situation, crossed the river with his infantry, probably at the extreme ends of his palisade, to support the cavalry. This pincer attack stopped the enemy from reorganizing and led to its flight.

A few days after the battle, and having ravaged the countryside, the Punic-Iberian army made its way to New Carthage. Thus ended the campaign in the north, an area that had never been part of the Carthaginian empire in Spain. Although the Carpetani were defeated, they would not be cowed, and rose to rebellion once again a few years after.

The Romans had defeated the Gauls by 221 BC, and refocused some of their energy towards a conflict between Saguntum and a neighbouring tribe of the Torboletae protected by Carthage. Rome used Saguntum to promote a hostile party to Carthage and create friction with the neighbouring tribe, thus undermining Carthaginian power south of the Ebro and exploiting Iberia's incredible mineral wealth. Hamilcar and Hasdrubal were not keen on a new fight with the Romans, and there is no evidence suggesting Hannibal envisioned an immediate war with Rome. The Carthaginian leadership in

North Africa and in Iberia were reminded of the Sicilian city of Messina, which had precipitated the First Punic War in 264 BC when its previously Punic-employed Mamertine mercenaries revolted and asked for Roman help. Similarly, Saguntum appealed repeatedly to Rome. In around 220/219 BC, Roman envoys arrived at Hannibal's headquarters in New Carthage perhaps hoping to bully the Punic leaders into submission, as they had done during the Truceless War. The envoys informed Hannibal and subsequently Carthage that Saguntum was under Roman protection and assumed they would again submit to their demands. Both in Iberia and at Carthage the Roman envoys were told they had no standing in the Saguntum affair. Carthage also upheld Hannibal's position despite the protests of Hanno, of the Peace Party, who sought good relations with Rome and desired to limit Carthaginian expansion to North Africa and not in Iberia. Hannibal's campaigns were not intended for offensives against Rome but rather were defensive in nature and limited to the Iberian Peninsula, in order to compensate for the enormous losses incurred during the previous two wars.

This wonderfully preserved relief is from a group known as the Sculptures of Osuna dated between 125–75 BC. It has been variously identified as Roman or Iberian. Note the greaves. Held in the National Archaeological Museum in Madrid. (Michelle Ricci)

Even though Carthage most likely sought peace, it was aware of Rome's bad faith in recent years. The desire to avoid challenging Rome directly may have also resulted in a lack of attention to the once-powerful Carthaginian war fleet. Without control of the mines in the Iberian Peninsula, Carthage might have faced extreme difficulties in paying the reparations owed to Rome, as well as recouping losses incurred from waging the First Punic and Truceless wars. Roman aggression throughout the Western Mediterranean was directed at Carthage. Rome was failing to honour its part of the Ebro treaty, and no doubt Saguntum would form the centre of gravity for Roman advances in Iberia to New Carthage, and could easily lead to Rome invading North Africa again. Perhaps Carthage recognized that ultimately there was to be a war with Rome. Perhaps they realized they had a fine commander who had expanded by diplomacy and by war Carthaginian interests in Iberia. To remain secure in exploiting commerce, Carthage needed to defend itself; but perhaps the best defence was to attack with all the advantages of manpower and wealth, and with

A bronze and silver buckle, along with remains of the iron rivets used to attach it to a leather belt. Small figurines show warriors wearing similar clasps, suggesting this was designed for use by a soldier. It is typical of a type of buckle produced in the central plain region of the Iberian Peninsula. It is closely related to engraved examples of artwork in Andalusia in the south-west of Spain, a province that strongly influenced the artistic development of the rest of Iberia. (The Met Museum)

Rome mired in potential other wars. Saguntum, like Messina, was the pivotal point on the path to war.

SAGUNTUM, 219 BC

The strategic situation for Carthage was simple. If Hannibal did not move on Saguntum, Rome would continue its interference in Iberia, and little would stop other tribes seeking Roman *fidum*, as Saguntum had. Hannibal may not have sought a war with Rome, but Saguntum represented the line drawn in the sand if Carthage wanted to retain its possessions in Iberia. A war with Rome was the last resort, pushed forward only by the threat to Carthaginian hegemony in Spain. Hannibal and the Carthaginian leadership in North Africa must have considered a potential conflict with Rome over Saguntum, yet it was far away from Roman power and thus would be fought with the advantage tilting to the Carthaginians. By taking the initiative, Hannibal would deny the Romans Saguntum as a base for their Iberian campaign. Perhaps Rome went to war fearing Hannibal's advance north of the Ebro.

In April or May of 219 BC, with Saguntum intransigent and pro-Carthaginian citizens having been killed, and cognizant of Rome's war with the Illyrians, Hannibal moved north. Saguntum was not a fortified village but a major city. It was situated on a steep 50m-high plateau, facing the sea and 1.6km (now 4km) from the coast. The city was 1km long from east to west but only about 100m wide, with its greatest weakness at the western wall, the point where Hannibal decided to attack. Hannibal divided his army into three units or areas of operation, each with a specific purpose.

Hannibal's siege of Saguntum, 219 BC

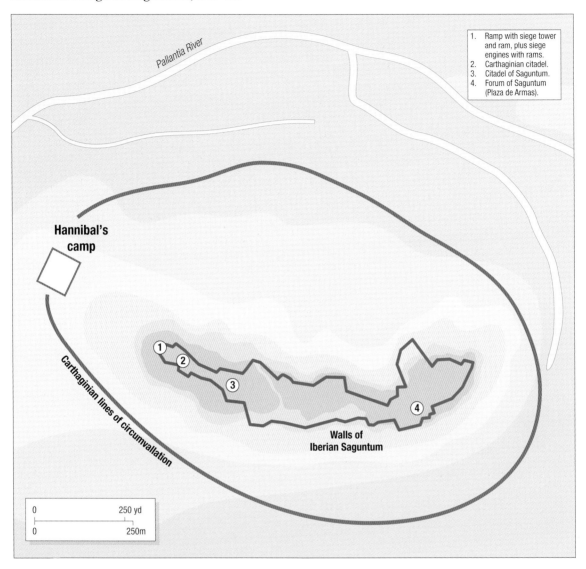

1. Ramp with siege tower and ram, plus siege engines with rams.
2. Carthaginian citadel.
3. Citadel of Saguntum.
4. Forum of Saguntum (Plaza de Armas).

Pallantia River

Hannibal's camp

Carthaginian lines of circumvallation

Walls of
Iberian Saguntum

| 0 | 250 yd |
| 0 | 250m |

Two units threw up lines of circumvallation to the north and south of Saguntum, comprising moats and palisades. The only area left open was to the west where Hannibal with his assault force had established his camp. An embankment was built to accommodate the use of siege towers and *vineae* (siege engines) with rams. The eastern side was too steep for an attack.

Polybius' narrative is short on details but rich in significance. He notes that seizing Saguntum would deprive Rome of a base to wage war in Iberia, that native tribes would fear the Punic war machine and that the seizure of the city would enable Hannibal to advance north without any resistance to his interior lines of communication. Saguntum would secure Hannibal abundant supplies, treasure for his troops and spoils for Carthage. Polybius notes: 'After a siege extending to the eighth month, in the course of which he endured every kind of suffering and anxiety, he finally succeeded in taking the town.' When the city was sacked, 'an immense booty in money, slaves

A depiction of a Roman army besieging a city. Note the massive siege tower and the breach in the wall. (New York Public Library)

and property fell into his hands. The money he reserved for the needs of his projected expedition; the slaves were distributed according to merit among his men; while the property was at once sent entire to Carthage.' Polybius believes the campaign was conducted ultimately to wage war against Rome.

Greater details of the siege are provided by Livy. He recounts the northern and southern circumvallation, and the western side where the walls and a tower were significantly taller than the rest of the city's fortification. Hannibal reportedly had a staggering 150,000 men available for the siege. Ramparts were built for siege engines and towers. During the clashes, Hannibal was seriously wounded when a javelin struck him in his thigh, leading to a blockade lasting a few days instead of a continued assault on Saguntum. Bearing in mind that siege weapons tended to be inaccurate, they were still effective. During the siege, assaults and repairs were ongoing. Following Hannibal's recovery, the renewed Punic attacks were fierce. The city was laid open when three towers collapsed and the two forces clashed in an open area between the crumbled wall and houses. The fighting was savage and foreshadowed Carthage's own brutal destruction in the Third Punic War.

Livy notes the use of the Saguntine weapon called the *phalarica*:

> a javelin with a shaft smooth and round up to the head, which, as in the *pilum*, was an iron point of square section. The shaft was wrapped in tow and then smeared with pitch; the iron head was 3ft [0.9m] long and capable of penetrating armour and body alike. Even if it only stuck in the shield and did not reach the body it was a most formidable weapon, for when it was discharged with the tow set on fire, the flame was fanned to a fiercer heat by its passage through the air, and it forced the soldier to throw away his shield and left him defenceless against the sword thrusts which followed.

The Saguntines drove the Carthaginian troops back to their encampment to the west of the city. Sometime after this, Roman envoys reached the harbour, but Hannibal denied them an audience, instead sending messengers to Carthage to prepare them for the arrival of the envoys sent from Rome.

The Carthaginian army safeguarded their siege engines while Hannibal gave them time to rest and recover from their hard-fought battles. The Saguntines repaired the damage to the best of their ability. Punic forces pushed forward a siege tower on rollers featuring *ballistae* (catapults) on each level, driving off the defenders from the wall and allowing 500 African troops to undermine the wall and successfully breach it. Hannibal ordered his siege machines forwards towards higher ground, where they enclosed the machines within a wall, creating a citadel-like structure. This may very well have been the *Arx* (citadel) Carthago (as opposed to the Saguntine citadel, which lay farther east into the city).

At a certain point, Hannibal suddenly left Saguntum with some of his forces to suppress the revolt of the Oretani and Carpetani, who had seized his recruiting officers. During his absence, Maharbal, son of Himilco, continued the operations with great success, using three battering rams to bring down more of the wall. Immediately upon Hannibal's return, the Punic forces assaulted the breach and captured part of Saguntum's citadel, where heavy clashes took place.

Sauguntum's repeated calls for Rome to honour its *fidum* remained unanswered. Rome was engaged in a war in the east and perhaps was about to enter another with Macedon. Saguntum was less important than Massilia to the north-east, and the safety of Roman interests elsewhere in the Mediterranean – yet, paradoxically, Saguntum would be seen by Rome as a cause for war.

When another defensive tower was knocked down, Punic forces poured into the city, and after a hard-fought battle defeated the by now demoralized and starved Saguntines in the eastern zone. This final slaughter happened in the Forum Saguntum (Plaza de Armas). All males (those who had not killed themselves by sword or fire) were executed, and a vast amount of treasure was secured. Hannibal then led his force from there to New Carthage for the winter, before entering Italy five months later.

Saguntum demonstrated to Hannibal and his staff the difficulties of siege warfare in the Iberian Peninsula. His subsequent rejection of a plan to attack Rome made sense, given that Rome enjoyed far greater local support and had control of the interior lines of communications, unlike the Saguntines. Saguntum and especially Rome were different to Arbucala, which was a heavily fortified settlement, but it, too, took time to reduce. Siege warfare was attritional, expending men and equipment, and especially time. Attention to logistics, critical to all campaigns, remained especially important during

A limestone sculpture known as the Lady of Elche, perhaps made in the 4th century BC, which may have been linked to the Carthaginian goddess Tanit. It was discovered in 1897 approximately 2km south of Elche, Spain, and is now located at the National Archaeological Museum, Madrid. (Cherine Bajjal)

Probably inspired by Celtic prototypes, and adopted by the Romans, Montefortino-type helmets were especially popular from the 4th to the 2nd centuries BC. This example is Etruscan. Originating from the Necropolis del Frontone, Perugia, it now is in the Museo Nazionale di Perugia, Italy. (The Met Museum)

sieges, and were easier to manage in Iberia, where the interior lines of communication were controlled; the subsequent Punic experiences in Italy would prove very different.

Hannibal's move south after the siege indicated that, despite the attack, he was honouring the Ebro treaty. He may very well have known that sacking Saguntum would increase friction with Rome, perhaps even leading to war. Strategically, Hannibal could have remained on the defensive, protecting Iberia and Carthage from anticipated Roman attacks. A long, drawn-out campaign meant Hannibal could be in only one place, but an attack into Italy would change the equation by breaking the allied confederation, reducing Roman manpower while causing internal rifts.

In the spring of 218 BC at New Carthage, Hannibal made final preparations for a war that was certain to come. Preparations must have taken at least two to three months, including the interchange of Iberian and African troops between Iberia and Carthage, perhaps to ensure loyalties but certainly to strengthen both places. Some 14,000 troops, 1,200 cavalry and 870 Balearic slingers were exchanged with an equal amount of African troops. No doubt alliances were being forged with the Celts that Hannibal would encounter along his route of march, especially the Celtic Boii in northern Italy, whom he would need to rely on for resupply and manpower once his tattered army descended from the Alps. Marching into Italy was Hannibal's only recourse: entrusting his army of invasion to the Punic navy would be a gamble, despite the various Punic landings during the subsequent war, given the likelihood of the Roman navy intercepting them.

Hannibal's Iberian troops were given furloughs and paid in silver coin, and last-minute operational plans were solidified while Hannibal visited Gadir, perhaps for divine guidance. His army was a veteran army born of the many campaigns in Iberia, with Iberians and North Africans at its core officered by Carthaginians. The Romans became aware of Hannibal's army reassembling in March 218 BC, which convinced them that he would most likely advance north of the Ebro. News of Carthaginians negotiating with Gallic tribes as far away as northern Italy gave Rome another reason to launch a war on Carthage with campaigns in Iberia and North Africa. At the heart of the Carthaginian strategy for the upcoming war was safeguarding Iberia and Carthage, and the use of envoys to weave alliances with allies.

Roman prestige and Carthage's unchallenged consolidation of territory south of the Ebro led Rome to send envoys in March 218 BC to Carthage in North Africa, demanding the surrender of Hannibal and those who had approved the attack on Saguntum. Any rejection would be cause for war, they stated. The Carthaginian senate repudiated the Roman demands, using the argument that the Barcid generals in Iberia had been legally as well as practically independent from their home state, and thus the Ebro accord did not bind them. The Roman envoys were sent away from Carthage without securing what they came for, which was probably what Rome expected to happen; Hannibal was not to be handed over to them.

Giovanni Battista Tiepolo's superb painting of the capture of Carthage in 146 BC. The painting shows the challenges of assaulting well-defended cities, as Hannibal experienced at Saguntum and the younger Scipio at New Carthage. (The Met Museum)

The Romans simultaneously had to deal with Demetrius of Pharos (c.300–214BC), who was attacking Illyrian cities under Roman protection, and they were also closely monitoring Philip V of Macedon (238–179 BC), who was embroiled in a war with the Aetolians and Spartans. However, renewed war with Carthage would be their foremost priority.

HANNIBAL DEPARTS SPAIN, 218 BC

Rome's naval superiority most likely drove Hannibal's plan to march north from Iberia, pass the Pyrenees and cross southern Gaul, traverse the Alps and head into the Po Valley in northern Italy. Hannibal's strategy emphasized the security of both Iberia and Carthage while taking the war onto Roman soil. To that end, Hannibal sent 20,000 Iberians to garrison Carthage. Carthage and Iberia were strongly held, twin centres of gravity, recognizing that Roman strategy would inevitably seek to attack both, which indeed it did.

Funding for Hannibal's grand campaign, providing both equipment and mercenaries, came from Iberia's mineral wealth. One Iberian mine alone provided 300lb of silver per day. According to Polybius, Hannibal's veteran army departed New Carthage with 90,000 infantry, 12,000 cavalry and 37 elephants. They left in early/mid-218 BC, probably in June, because the receding water levels of rivers made it easier to cross them, and also because the arrival of the harvest season eased the logistical requirements of feeding so large an army. Hannibal marched in three columns to ease the burden on logistics. The distance from Hannibal's base at New Carthage to the Ebro River was 462km, which his army covered in roughly five weeks. Beyond it lay hostile territories which they first had to force to submit. Crossing the

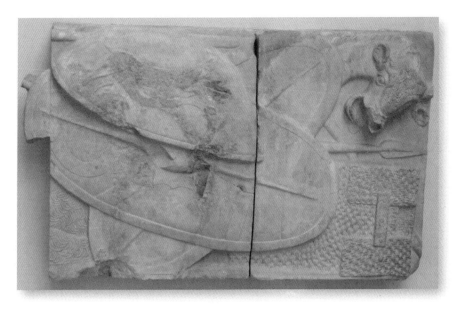

An image from the Pergamon (Bergama, Turkey) exhibit in Berlin's Pergamon Museum showing an oval-shaped shield and mail shirt. Pergamon was allied with Rome against Macedon.

Ebro, the Punic boundary of the Iberian Peninsula, was to Hannibal the point of no return, just as crossing the Rubicon would be to Gaius Julius Caesar (110–44 BC) on his way to end the Roman Republic in 49 BC.

Hannibal left Punic Iberia under the command of his brother Hasdrubal. According to Polybius, who 'found on Lacinium [a promontory at Capo della Colonne in present-day Calabria] a bronze tablet which Hannibal had caused to be inscribed with these particulars when he was in Italy', Hasdrubal's command was as follows:

> Fifty quinqueremes, two quadriremes and five triremes, 32 of the quinqueremes being furnished with crews, and all five of the triremes; also cavalry consisting of 450 Libyophenicians and Libyans, 300 Lergetae, 1,800 Numidians of the Massolian, Massaesylian, Maccoeian and Maurian tribes, who dwell by the ocean; with 11,850 Libyans, 300 Ligures, 500 of the Balearic islanders and 21 elephants.

The Carthaginian navy in Spain had to defend its possessions and be able to continue trade with Carthage in North Africa. Later, Hasdrubal was to raise a larger army and follow in his older brother's footsteps into Italy.

It took Hannibal 2½ months to subdue the tribes in northern Iberia, although he failed to take Tarraco and Emporion along the north-eastern seaboard. As he continued to advance north from Emporion in August 218 BC, Hannibal detached one of his officers, Hanno, with an 11,000-strong army to maintain control over the rebellious tribes in his absence. His other task was to halt potential Roman advances in the north of the Iberian Peninsula and also to provide a logistical base for Hasdrubal's army's anticipated march into Italy the following year.

Hannibal's grand army experienced major reductions in force throughout its advance. First, there was Hanno's detachment of 11,000, and then losses of 3,000 Spanish deserters and 7,000 Iberians (Livy says all were Carpetani) who were released home – in total, 21,000 men from his ranks. These additional losses amounted to 20,000 infantry and 1,000 cavalry. When Hannibal set out to cross the Pyrenees, his army had been further reduced

to 50,000 foot, 9,000 cavalry and 37 elephants – out of 90,000 foot and 12,000 cavalry. Perhaps some of these were for garrisons left to protect his lines of communication and to serve as additional logistics bases for Hasdrubal's army. By the time Hannibal's grand army reached the Rhone in France, it had shrunk by a further 12,000 infantry and 1,000 cavalry, reducing the Punic-Iberian force to 38,000 and 8,000 respectively, but still retained 37 elephants. Losses had to be expected during the planning phases of the campaign, not just to combat but also to garrison duties, desertion, illness and natural deaths. Whether or not the planners had accounted for so large a number is unknown, although Polybius' numbers may be incorrect.

Fortunately for Hannibal, the Celts of the Boii and Insubres ambushed a Roman legion in northern Italy, forcing the consular army intended for the elder Scipio and Iberia to be redirected there, leaving Scipio to raise a new consular army for service in the Iberian Peninsula. By the time the two new legions had been raised and had made their way to the allied city of Massilia to launch their attack on Hannibal in Iberia, the elder Scipio discovered Hannibal was near the Rhone and not in Iberia. The legions arrived a few days after the Carthaginians had crossed the river, encountering only rear elements of the Punic cavalry.

The elder Scipio's stark realization of Hannibal's intentions to wage war in Italy by crossing the Alps forced him to make a difficult decision. Should he return to Italy with his consular army, abandoning Rome's strategy of wresting Iberia from Carthage? Or should he reinforce Rome with his army? He decided to stick with Rome's strategy, sending his two newly raised legions to Iberia under the command of his brother Gnaeus Cornelius Scipio Calvus, who would serve in the Iberian Peninsula from 218 BC until his death seven years later. The decision to send in the consular army had far-reaching implications for the war as a whole, since Iberia was crucial for the funding and manpower it provided to Hannibal's army. Rome, and the elder Scipio, had a high degree of confidence that Hannibal needed time to reach Italy. Rome would be able to engage him in the spring of 217 BC without the help of the two legions destined for Iberia. The elder Scipio's consular army was most vital in the Iberian theatre of operations. There, it would not only challenge

Carthage for dominion of the mineral and agricultural wealth, but it would also reduce Carthaginian hegemony over the native tribes, and tie down any reinforcements destined for Hannibal.

It took Hannibal's Punic-Iberian army five gruelling months to reach the Po Valley from New Carthage, and although challenging, in all likelihood they followed trails long established by regional tribes during their Alpine crossings. Nonetheless, it had been audacious to strike at Rome overland. The crossing was difficult, with continuous attacks by native tribes and challenging environmental factors. By the time the Carthaginians descended into the Po Valley to recover from its arduous march, Hannibal's army numbered around 20,000 foot, composed of 12,000 African and 8,000 Iberian troops, 6,000 horse and all of his 37 elephants. It was a small army, but Hannibal was hopeful it would be reinforced by Celts and former Roman allies. It was a masterstroke, throwing Roman strategy to the wind, forcing Rome to abandon simultaneous twin attacks on Carthage and Punic Iberia. Instead, Rome had to switch to the defensive to ensure survival on home territory; an attack on Carthage was out of the question. The initiative lay with Hannibal, and it would take years for Rome to recover from this. Spain thus became a secondary theatre of operations, with the Romans seeking to slow the flow of Carthaginian reinforcements and funding while tackling previously unhindered operations against native tribes.

THE BATTLE OF CISSA, 218 BC

In the autumn of 218 BC, the elder Scipio's consular army was based at Emporion, a Greek colony established by Massilia, on the north-eastern Iberian shoreline near the Pyrenees, which served as a naval base and winter quarters. The consular army comprised two Roman legions of 8,000 legionaries, 600 Roman *equites*, 14,000 allied foot and 1,600 horses, numbering in total 24,200 men. Scipio's force was supported by 60 quinqueremes, which controlled the north-eastern seaboard. By making several unopposed landings along the shore, he gained control of the area from Emporion to Tarraco (Tarragona). Polybius said: 'When he had garrisoned those towns on the coast that submitted, he led his whole army inland, having by this time a not inconsiderable contingent of Iberian allies; and took possession of the towns on his line of march, some by negotiation and some by force of arms.' The latter included sieges of fortified settlements.

Unlike Gnaeus' singular consular army with its ranks filled by Iberian allies, the Carthaginian army was spread out over large territories requiring not only administration but also a military presence to subdue potential regional revolts. Since large armies require supplies of food, the Carthaginian operational plan called for the division of its army into smaller field forces, spreading them throughout their territories. One of the disadvantages for their overall command was the great distance between each. Although they could count on secure interior lines of communication, armies needed to be organized, logistics needed to be addressed and distances had to be covered on foot. Unless timely intelligence was on hand, the unexpected arrival of an enemy force could prove challenging. If Carthaginian field forces were able to unite, they certainly would outnumber or at least equal the Romans in size, and would use their superior knowledge of the terrain to their benefit.

The Roman invasion of the Iberian Peninsula from Emporion had caught Hanno and also Hasdrubal, the overall commander, off guard. When it occurred, Hanno, whose troops were guarding Hannibal's massive baggage train, was caught well south of Emporion dealing with an insurrection. His task to thwart any Roman advances failed. The Carthaginians had not been able to prevent the Roman naval landings. Hanno had not even been aware of the Roman movements, made easier by seaborne operations, until it was too late. Dealing with rebellion to the south and the size of the consular army was beyond his army's capability. If Hanno had been aware of the potential for Roman naval assaults, he may have been able to throw them off the beaches before the legions fully deployed. Instead, Hanno was forced to withdraw inland to a more hospitable region, supported by allied Iberians, while Hasdrubal speed-marched with 8,000 foot and 1,000 cavalry from New Carthage north. What followed formed the first clash between Romans and Carthaginians on the Iberian Peninsula.

Hanno's army settled at the fortified town of Cissa (Valls, Catalonia), to the north-east and inland of Tarraco, where it built a military camp. Modern excavations at the site have revealed a moat that may have been 40m wide and 5m deep, with an overall length of nearly 500m; the Punic-Iberian army may have built a moat around Cissa, or the remains discovered may have been previously dug by its inhabitants. Although Hanno raised a local levy, his army of 10,000 infantry and 1,000 cavalry was vastly outnumbered by the elder Scipio's consular army of more than 24,000 Roman and allied foot, not counting the large numbers of Iberian allies who had joined the Romans since their invasion.

Hanno had two options, each with its own unique challenges. He could remain in his fortified camp, hoping to withstand assault or siege while waiting for Hasdrubal's army to cover the 600km from New Carthage to Cissa (which would have taken time, even with the army speed-marching between 30 and 50km per day). If he could hold out against the Roman assault, the combined armies of Hanno and Hasdrubal could achieve numerical parity. The advantage then might lie with the Punic commanders as they were experienced in battle, knowledgeable of the terrain and had established relationships with the Iberians. The Roman-allied Iberians might also desert upon Hasdrubal's arrival. The other option for Hanno was to offer battle near Cissa, with his camp and town to his back. He chose battle, even though it seemed wiser to remain behind his fortifications. The decision to take on a vastly superior army must have come from news that, with the arrival of the Romans, various native tribes were stirred up and ready to revolt against the Carthaginians. Hanno had just dealt with one

A Phoenician ceramic amphora from the 3rd century BC with the form of a woman/deity. It was found at the BeniAsl necropolis, in Bizerte, Tunisia, and is now in the Bardo National Museum.

A bronze helmet of the Montefortino type, held at the British Museum, London, UK.

such rebellion. The longer he waited, the more the native peoples became restless and joined the Romans, who had already subjugated and recruited Iberians along the coast, and the more the balance tipped in favour of the Romans. Hasdrubal was many days, if not weeks, away. Although Hanno's army had combat experience from their Iberian campaigns the previous years, it was numerically inferior by one-half. The consular army was an unknown to the Carthaginians. For Hanno, battle it was.

We know the battle was fought near the town of Cissa. Our only source for details of the fighting comes from the Roman general and writer Sextus Julius Frontinus (AD 40–103). In his *Stratagems*, he states the Carthaginian battle line was composed of two main groups: the Iberians were on the right wing, while the Africans were on the left. We must assume that they equally shared the centre of the line. We also know the terrain was flat; the only high ground, consisting of the Padres Mountains, rose to the west of the town. The Iberians, Frontinus writes, were considered sturdy soldiers, but with typical Roman propaganda claims that they fought for others (i.e. as mercenaries), and thus were not of the same moral calibre as Roman citizen soldiers, who fought for their city. The Iberians may have been mercenaries, but they were fighting on their own soil against an invader who did not enjoy long-established relationships, in contrast with the Carthaginians. The Africans may have been 'lesser fighters', but were more resolute; what made them so, Frontinus does not tell us, but we assume he meant less resolute in character and steadfastness. Yet African troops demonstrated their fighting prowess repeatedly throughout the Punic Wars, and the Africans had subjugated Iberia over the decades, even if their armies were supplemented with Iberian natives.

The tactic Gnaeus employed here was well known in ancient history (as between Boeotians and Spartans at Leuctra in 371 BC): an echelon formation attack. In essence, Gnaeus held back his left wing (presumably, allied legions) at an angle, thus not engaging the Iberians opposite them, in effect refusing his left flank, while the right advanced and sought combat. The Roman right wing was loaded with his best troops, and here we assume they comprised Roman legionaries and not allied troops. The Roman right advanced and clashed with the Africans opposite them while pinning Hanno's Iberians with their left wing, which was close enough to advance and attack should they manoeuvre to battle. Gnaeus and his Roman right wing defeated the African left wing and put them to flight, allowing for his entire consular army to then focus on Hanno's Iberian wing, which had not been engaged in battle but were mercly spectators, forcing them to surrender. Punic casualties were said to have been 6,000 killed in action and 2,000 prisoners, out of 11,000 soldiers. The bulk of the dead must have come from the Africans, since they were the ones engaged in combat, while the majority of the captured were therefore Iberians, even if the numbers seem unreasonably high.

Frontinus tells us: 'After the battle, the Romans raided a nearby Carthaginian camp, located on the edge of a town, and destroyed everything.'

Archaeological findings in the moat contained coins and lead projectiles, so clearly some fighting occurred in this area, too. Hanno was captured along with the local Ilergetae chief Andobales (Indibilis), together with all the stores and military equipment of Hannibal's baggage train. Andobales, according to Polybius, 'was a despot of central Iberia and had always been inclined to the side of Carthage. Defeating this army in a pitched battle, Gnaeus not only got possession of a rich booty, for the whole baggage of the army invading Italy had been left under its charge, but secured the friendly alliance of all the Iberian tribes north of the Iber [Ebro].' It was a crucial victory for Rome.

The speed of the Roman march had surprised the Carthaginians, much like Hannibal's march to the Alps had surprised Rome's leadership. Hasdrubal marched with speed from New Carthage but arrived too late. He was, however, able to slaughter great numbers of the Roman naval contingents on the beaches north of the Ebro, forcing them to their ships. It was a minor victory.

After the battle, Gnaeus left a modest garrison at Tarraco and returned with his fleet to Emporion for winter quarters.

A bronze Etruscan helmet with cheek guards, dating from around the mid-4th century BC. (The Met Museum)

Hasdrubal then instigated a revolt by the Ilergetae, who had given hostages to Scipio. He then laid waste to the nearby land, forcing Gnaeus out of his winter quarters. Having caused significant damage to Roman interests, Hasdrubal then retreated south of the Ebro, and employed himself in fortifying and garrisoning the posts south of the river, taking up his winter quarters at New Carthage.

Gnaeus took Hasdrubal's absence to punish the Ilergetae, who had fled to the safety of their capital of Athanàgia. Recent archaeological discoveries provide details of Athanàgia (Lat. Atanagrum, modern Molí d'Espígol). The city was situated on a gentle hill, and surrounded by large defensive walls faced with smooth stone that were 2.1m thick and almost 5m high in some places. Two defensive towers and fortifications have also been discovered. The Romans besieged the town for but a few days, as the Ilergetae soon surrendered and handed over more hostages to Scipio along with reparations. The Ilergetae were once again under Roman hegemony and caused no further problems until 212 BC. The city was abandoned around the year 200 BC as a consequence of the Second Punic War.

The Romans next focused on the Carthaginian allies of the Ausetani near the Ebro. The Romans besieged the town and fought off an ambush by the Lacetani, a neighbouring tribe seeking to aid the besieged Ausetani. The consular army slew 12,000 of them according to Livy, with the survivors dispersing across the country:

> The blockade continued for 30 days, during which the snow scarce ever lay less deep than 4ft [1.2m]; and it had covered to such a degree the sheds and mantelets of the Romans, that it alone served as a defence when fire was frequently thrown on them by the enemy. At last, when Amusitus, their leader, had fled to Hasdrubal, they surrendered, on condition of paying 20 talents of silver.

The elder Scipio rejoined his fleet, and took up winter quarters at Tarraco, bringing his campaign to a successful conclusion. The significance of the Roman victories at the Ebro and elsewhere meant that 'the Romans were then in control of the territory to the north of the Ebro, while the Carthaginians established their bases to the south'. In under two months Gnaeus was able to wrest territories north of the Ebro from the Carthaginians and establish a base vital for future operations in Tarraco.

Where Hasdrubal and other Carthaginian commanders had failed in the Iberian Peninsula, Hannibal outshone them all with his victories in Italy. In 218 BC, a cavalry clash at the Battle of Ticinus in late November witnessed the first Carthaginian victory. In this battle, the elder Scipio, who had returned to Italy after sending Gnaeus and his legion on to Iberia, was badly wounded and was reportedly saved by his 16-year-old son, the younger Scipio. A month later, in late December, Hannibal destroyed a Roman army under Tiberius Sempronius Longus, which had been sent as reinforcements to the northern front, at the Battle of Trebia. In June 217 BC, another Roman army of four legions under Gaius Flaminius was annihilated at Lake Trasimene.

THE NAVAL ENGAGEMENT AT THE EBRO, 217 BC

The lower reaches of the Ebro River were important during the early stages of the war between 218 and 212 BC. It comes as no surprise that a Roman camp had been built on the northern bank of the river near Palma (Tarraco, modern Tarragona) to intercept routes travelling north and south along the coast, as well as to control sea traffic off its delta. Archaeological finds indicate the presence of a military camp – possibly the Roman camp known as Nova Classis mentioned by Livy.

Ready to seize the initiative against the Romans in the early summer of 217 BC, Hasdrubal led an attack on land, supported by a 40-ship navy under the command of Himilco. Hasdrubal marched on Tarraco by crossing the Ebro and making camp near its delta, supported by his warships. The Roman consul Gnaeus thought of advancing against his Carthaginian counterpart, but instead, and perhaps worried by the prospect of a land battle, chose to place his best fighters on his ships and sailed towards the Carthaginian navy, halting 16km short of the Ebro delta. From there, two Massiliote ships conducted a reconnaissance, and returned to inform Gnaeus of the Carthaginian positions. Hasdrubal had encamped near the banks of the Ebro while the fleet was stationed at the mouth of the river.

Gnaeus decided to attack with his fleet, hoping to catch the Carthaginians off guard. His advance was successful, until the Roman fleet was spotted by guards at one of several coastal watchtowers. The arrival of the Romans threw the Punic-Iberians into disarray. Hasdrubal ordered the fleet to deploy, sending mounted messengers to hastily assemble various sailors and marines from the surrounding beach while he readied his infantry to give support from the coast. The Punic forces had been surprised, and hurriedly manning the ships was fraught with difficulties, as Livy records:

> The Carthaginians, therefore, thrown into disorder, not more by the enemy and the battle than by their own tumult, having rather made an attempt at fighting than commenced a battle, turned their fleet for flight; and as the mouth of the river which was before them could not be entered in so broad a line, and by so many pressing in at the same time, they ran their ships on shore in every part. And being received, some in the shallows, and others on the dry shore, some armed and some unarmed, they escaped to their friends, who were drawn up in battle-array over the shore. Two Carthaginian ships were captured and four sunk on the first encounter.

Others abandoned their ships and sought refuge with the Carthaginian forces on the shore.

Polybius ascribes the reason for the Roman victory to a lack of Carthaginian desire to clash in arms:

> But, after engaging, the Carthaginians made but a short struggle for victory, and very soon gave way. For the support of the troops on the beach did less service in encouraging them to attack, than harm in offering them a safe place of retreat. Accordingly, after losing two ships with their crews, and the oars and marines of four others, they gave way and made for the land; and when the Romans pressed on with spirit in pursuit, they ran their ships ashore, and leaping from the vessels fled for refuge to the troops. The Romans came boldly close to land, towed off such of the vessels as could be got afloat, and sailed away in great exultation at having beaten the enemy at the first blow, secured the mastery of the sea, and taken 25 of the enemy's ships.

In contrast, the Roman-Massiliote fleet's success was attributed to the superiority of the Massiliote sailors and the disarray of the Carthaginian crews. The Roman naval victory crushed Punic sea power for good. Gnaeus sailed to New Carthage immediately after the victory, where he raided its outer zones, returning to Tarraco with much loot.

After the defeat, Hasdrubal had no choice but to retreat to New Carthage in the autumn of 217 BC to consolidate his army and the territories below the Ebro River. North of it, the Romans were in control, in effect blocking any support to Hannibal in Italy. The Roman presence went far beyond its original footprint.

The sea battle at the Ebro River conclusively established Roman naval superiority, limiting the Punic fleet to raids throughout the war. On one occasion, 70 ships from Carthage attempted to support Hannibal by sailing around Sardinia to Pisa, but the fleet withdrew – just as news of victory at Lake Trasimene spread – when 120 Roman warships approached. On another occasion, one Roman convoy was successfully sunk by the Carthaginian fleet en route to Spain.

With the success at the Ebro, and with clear sea lanes, Rome ordered the elder Scipio with 20 ships and 8,000 reinforcements to join his older brother Gnaeus in Spain. Rome's campaign in the Iberian Peninsula was enjoying success, offsetting the low morale caused by its devastating defeats at the hands of Hannibal in Italy.

The following year, 216 BC, the united Scipio brothers and an army of 30,000 marched south-west of the Ebro, advancing as far as Saguntum, in order to win over more native tribes. The appointed Carthaginian commander Bostar was to prevent Roman incursion south-west of the Ebro, but he could do very little in the face of overwhelming force and he withdrew to Saguntum. Hasdrubal was busy reducing a rebellion by the Turdetani around the Baetis River. The Scipio brothers advanced 160km to Saguntum, accompanied at sea by their naval forces. However, they became concerned about besieging the city because of their extended lines of communication and the possibility of a strong Carthaginian army under Hasdrubal advancing against them; so, the Romans withdrew again to their winter quarters in Tarraco. The result so far favoured the Roman side, as they had secured Iberia north of the Ebro, they controlled the seas and they had been able to undermine loyalties of some local tribes south of the Ebro. The war in Iberia, however, now ground to a halt.

On the Italian mainland, Hannibal was victorious at Cannae in 216 BC, slaughtering tens of thousands of legionaries, *equites* and senators.

It was a stunning victory for Hannibal and a huge setback for Rome. Hannibal's younger brother and brilliant cavalry commander Mago brought news of the tremendous victory to Carthage, leading to a subtle change in strategy. Carthage now planned to extend the war simultaneously along many fronts. Hannibal was to continue to split off Roman-allied cities and crush Rome's legions with reinforcements promised for his theatre of operations; meanwhile, Punic forces were to push Roman troops out of Iberia, regain Sardinia and reestablish themselves in Sicily in order to regain dominance over the Western Mediterranean. To that end, an alliance was made with Macedon, which resented Roman intrusion into and control of Illyria.

Hasdrubal received orders from Carthage to march with all haste to Italy to reinforce and finish the campaign that had gone beyond the best of hopes. The challenge for Hasdrubal was twofold, as Livy notes:

The report of [Hasdrubal's departure], spreading over Iberia, made almost all the states declare for the Romans. Accordingly, [Hasdrubal] wrote immediately to Carthage, to inform them how much mischief the report of his march had produced. That if he really did leave Iberia, the Romans would be masters of it all before he could pass the Iberus [Ebro]. For, besides that he had neither an army nor a general whom he could leave to supply his place, so great were the abilities of the Roman generals who commanded there, that they could scarcely be opposed with equal forces. If, therefore, they had any concern for preserving Iberia, they ought to send a general with a powerful army to succeed him.

A drawing by French artist Étienne-Pierre-Adrien Gois (1731–1823) showing Hannibal before the senate of Carthage. Beside him, a figure empties a vessel, spilling rings or jewelry onto the ground; after the Battle of Cannae, Mago returned to Carthage with the rings of all the Roman senators and *equites* that had been killed. (The Met Museum)

To make matters more complicated, the fleet that had failed at the sea battle at the Ebro was ordered to prepare for new operations. Instead, a mutiny of its captains also instigated a rebellion of the Tartessi (north of Gades), which kept Hasdrubal busy in 216 BC. Constant rebellions in the Iberian Peninsula and at home in Carthage by Numidian tribes were a continual distraction and impacted on Carthaginian strategy.

Nonetheless, buoyed by victory at Cannae and with the new strategy in mind, Hasdrubal took to the offensive in 215 BC, having been reinforced from Carthage with 4,000 infantry and 1,000 cavalry. Another army, under Himilco, was also sent to Iberia to handle Iberian affairs in Hasdrubal's absence and to control the rebellious southern region Hasdrubal had previously defeated; this finally allowed him free rein to advance against the Scipio brothers entrenched in the north and blocking the route to Hannibal and to victory.

A quarter shekel minted in Punic Iberia sometime between 237 and 209 BC. The obverse features a laureate male head facing left with a club over his far shoulder, and the reverse an elephant advancing right. (Classical Numismatic Group, Inc. http://www.cngcoins.com)

The Scipio brothers were laying siege to Dertosa (also known as Hibera, modern Tortosa), a wealthy town on the west bank of the Ebro, when in mid-summer 215 BC they heard of the Carthaginian advance against them. Hasdrubal, instead of aiding the besieged town, forced the Romans to end their operations by besieging an Iberian town allied to the Romans. The stage for a crucial battle was set: a Carthaginian victory would deal a fatal blow to Rome by allowing Hasdrubal to significantly reinforce his brother in Italy.

THE BATTLE OF DERTOSA, 215 BC

The Battle of Dertosa saw two nearly equal-strength armies face one another. Although not involved in the battle, the Roman fleet supported the consular army during its land operations. Under the command of the elder Scipio, it comprised at least 30 ships, if not more than three times that number when adding the original 60 that Gnaeus had arrived in, the 30 of the elder Scipio's army and the number of Carthaginian ships captured at the Ebro, as well as an unknown number of Massiliote warships.

The Carthaginian army was composed of various tribes and ethnicities: Iberians, Celt-Iberians and North African peoples including Carthaginians and Liby-Phoenicians. Most had gained combat experience against native tribes in Iberia and North Africa and perhaps against the Romans themselves, but only in minor clashes. Employing a similar tactic used by Hannibal at the Trebia and Cannae, Hasdrubal's Iberians were in the centre and his Liby-Phoenician African troops (Livy calls them Carthaginians) on the right wing supported by Numidian cavalry to their front. Livy also writes that the Numidians, unusually perhaps, had two horses each, which they switched when one became tired. The Punic left wing was composed of levy, African and mercenary troops. To their front was most likely the Carthaginian-Iberian line cavalry. The elephants were almost certainly placed behind the cavalry. Hasdrubal's army numbered close to that of the consular army's 30,000 men.

An example of a well-preserved Montefortino-type helmet held at the Los Angeles County Museum of Art.

The consular army, undefeated in three years of campaigning, was in its traditional triple deployment of line infantry. The *velites* were stationed among the first line of the Romans, but also with the second behind the standards. We presume this to be in front and behind the *hastati*, and before the *principes* and *triarii*. Roman and allied cavalry guarded the flanks. The number of native troops supporting the Romans is unknown.

The key to victory for the Carthaginians lay in their centre being able to withstand the Roman assault while the wings enveloped the Roman army in a by now well-known double-encirclement. At the Trebia, 10,000 Romans survived by cutting through Hannibal's centre; at Cannae they did not succeed in doing so, resulting in their complete annihilation. However, in this battle the Punic cavalry may have been in front of the wings, perhaps intending to hide the movement of the infantry flanks; or perhaps, in typical fashion, they deployed not in front of the wings but to their sides, with the elephants behind them. The latter seems more likely.

Neither army was superior, but in the traditionally biased Roman narrative the legionaries were patriotic and willing to conquer or die for Rome, while the enemy was less determined and composed mostly of Iberians, who preferred to die on home soil rather than, having achieved victory, being forced to march to, and die in, Italy serving their Punic overlords. The Iberian tribes fought well for the Carthaginians, be that in the campaigns in Iberia, North Africa, Italy or while crossing the Alps and fighting off Celtic tribes. At Cannae, they proved their mettle fighting alongside Hannibal and Mago, who manned the crucial centre with them, winning a stunning victory.

The armies faced one another and minor skirmishing took place, until signals for battle were given for both armies to advance onto the plain. The battle opened with an exchange of javelins, whereupon the Iberian-held centre immediately gave ground, showing their backs, and allowing the Romans to press forwards. The wings witnessed cavalry clashes as both Punic detachments charged their Roman counterparts (presumably simultaneously), with the Romans 'exposed in a twofold attack'. Somehow, the Romans united in the centre of the battle line, creating sufficient strength to force the Punic wings to disperse in different directions and prompting two separate battles on the field. In effect, the consular army without great difficulty pushed the retreating Iberians off the field and then turned on each Carthaginian wing to create two separate clashes, in which the Romans now held numerical superiority. Once Hasdrubal's cavalry wings noticed the withdrawal of their centre, they fled the battlefield, driving their elephants before them. The cavalry clashes must have been minimal since everything fell apart early on. At the very last moment, Hasdrubal fled the field with his treasury intact and the majority of the Iberian troops and most, if not all, of the cavalry and elephants. The Romans set to plundering the nearby Carthaginian camp.

Had the Scipio brothers lost at Dertosa, they would have been forced to retreat, if not withdraw completely, from Iberia while Hasdrubal would have been able to reinforce his brother Hannibal in Italy. After the Punic defeat, more Iberian tribes joined the Romans. The Carthaginian situation in Iberia itself was perilous, although not catastrophic, because Hasdrubal still had funds and his army had not been destroyed. Rome received the news of this great victory as a tonic for its bitter losses suffered at the hands of Hannibal, who was master of most of Italy at the time.

The figures are part of a group of limestone reliefs known as the Sculptures of Osuna, dated between 125–75 BC. One of the men is holding a small round shield. He also wears some form of armour. The other seems to wear a simple tunic. Held in the National Archaeological Museum in Madrid. (Michelle Ricci)

A NEW STRATEGY

In 215 BC, Mago, who had accompanied Hannibal to Italy, was sent to Carthage to raise a new army of 12,000 foot, 1,500 cavalry and 20 elephants, supported by 60 ships. Mago's army was to land at Locri (Calabria, Italy)

Panoramic photo from Rhonda showing the challenging terrain sometimes encountered during the Second Punic War. (Michelle Ricci)

while Hasdrubal was to march to northern Italy. This strategy would see Hannibal controlling mainland Italy and acting as the anvil to Mago's hammer. This was in addition to Carthage's attempt to spread the war throughout the Mediterranean. The overall situation, however, had shifted. Mago's new army was instead ordered to Iberia following the recent Roman victories there, which were endangering the overall plan of attack. An additional 20,000 infantry and 4,000 horsemen were to be recruited in Iberia for operations in the peninsula and in Italy. Simultaneously, Carthage ordered 4,000 Numidians and 400 elephants to be sent as a reinforcement to Hannibal, along with many talents of silver.

In the summer of 215 BC a small Punic army landed at Locri, having avoided the Roman fleet near Sicily. The Sardinian operation under Hasdrubal the Bald, on the other hand, misfired when a storm threw his fleet off course, allowing Rome to deal with the island's rebels and reinforce its sole legion there. Hasdrubal the Bald's army then landed and organized itself, but was defeated in battle and its commander captured. The remnants of the army sailed back for home, running into a Roman fleet that had been raiding North Africa, losing seven ships and seeing the rest of the fleet scattered. Meanwhile, Syphax, king of the Masaesyli of western Numidia, formed an alliance with Rome and rebelled against Carthage, requiring Hasdrubal and some of his army to return from Iberia to North Africa, where Carthage won a decisive battle around 213 BC. An alliance with Macedon, however, was successful, and Rome now had to worry about a potential war with the Greeks at the behest of Macedon. In Sicily, Carthage hoped to embroil Roman forces once again as it had done in the summer of 215 BC. Ultimately, the multi-front strategy forced Rome into recruiting slaves and criminals into its legions to fill manpower.

Things were on a knife edge for Rome despite its victories in Iberia. The victory by the Scipio brothers over Hasdrubal at Dertosa witnessed shifts in allegiances of the Celt-Iberian tribes, who had provided hardened swordsmen to Carthage. Reinforcements brought by Mago's arrival sought to redress the imbalance. Hasdrubal's distraction caused by the war against Syphax in North Africa allowed the Romans to make progress from 214 to 212 BC in the Iberian Peninsula. The Romans advanced into the heart of Carthaginian territory there when they crossed the Ebro and captured Saguntum in 212 BC, six years after its sack by Hannibal. The Carthaginian stronghold of Castulo in the valley of the Upper Baetis also surrendered to the Scipio brothers. Hannibal had married a royal woman from Castulo, so the subjugation of the town must have been particularly upsetting. Rome had conquered approximately one-third of Punic Iberia during those years. These events boosted the morale and war effort of Rome following its numerous defeats in Italy and Sicily. The victories were crucial for the continuation of Rome's strategy of eventually taking the war to North Africa.

The successful conclusion by Carthage of the war against Syphax in North Africa led to renewed efforts to reclaim Iberia and to drive the Romans out of the peninsula. To that end, three Punic armies were dispatched. In 212 BC, Hasdrubal returned with an army, Mago raised a further one that included Masinissa and his excellent Numidian cavalry, and a third army arrived under the command of Hasdrubal, son of Gisco. Opposing them were the two legions of the consular army reinforced by 20,000 Celt-Iberian troops. Until Hasdrubal's arrival in 212 BC, most of the territories lacked Carthaginian field forces, and because of that weakness, the Scipio brothers had been able to split their army into two, easing logistical requirements and allowing them to manoeuvre independently in wider areas of the territory. The elder Scipio was at Castulo on the Upper Baetis while Gnaeus was headquartered in Osuna (Urso, Seville) in the hinterland of New Carthage.

THE UPPER BAETIS, 211 BC

Following news of Hasdrubal's arrival, coupled with his orders for Indibilis and other friendly chieftains to raise troops, and possibly the fickleness of native troops, the Romans suffered large numbers of Iberian deserters. The two Roman armies were also kept apart because of the locations of the opposing field forces, which made reuniting the consular army difficult. Eventually, two battles would be fought, with twin engagements at Castulo first then at Ilorca – collectively they are referred to as the Battle of the Upper Baetis.

The Roman commander the elder Scipio was caught off guard when his camp was subjected to harassment and raiding day and night by Masinissa and his Numidian cavalry The Numidians were so audacious they even rode up to the camp gate, charging the guards and sowing confusion and fear among the soldiers. Masinissa's cavalry wreaked havoc and charged the ramparts so often that Livy compared it to the Romans being under siege. When erecting a marching camp, the Romans normally dug out a 1–1.5m-deep ditch around their camp using spades and other tools, forming ramparts with the excavated soil, on top of which they put up a palisade made of sharpened stakes they carried during the campaign.

The elder Scipio received intelligence indicating greater problems. The Iberian chieftain Indibilis, commanding 7,500 Suessetani, a tribe located north of the Ebro near Tarraco, neighbouring the Ilergetae, was to join Mago's force. Publius made a plan to attack and intercept the Iberians at night before they could unite with Mago, hoping to render his position untenable. A unified Punic force would pin down the Romans, allowing time for other forces to join the Carthaginians. The elder Scipio took charge of the operation and left legate Tiberius Fonteius to guard the camp. To escape detection by the ever-marauding Numidians, and to close on and destroy the approaching enemy, the elder Scipio decided on a night march, and they departed their camp at midnight.

The Upper Baetis, 211 BC: Castulo and Ilorca

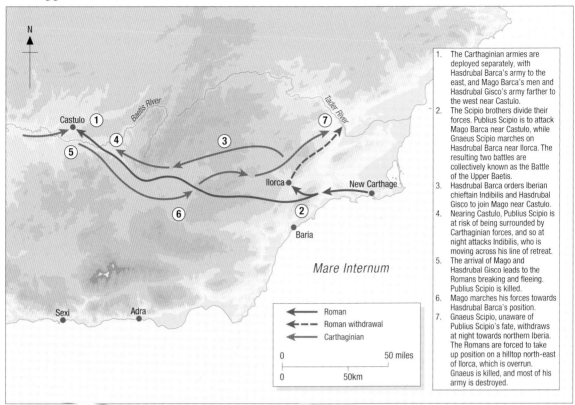

Castulo ①

Baetis River

Tader River

④

⑤

③

⑦

Ilorca ●

New Carthage ●

②

⑥

Baria ●

Mare Internum

Sexi ●   Adra ●

← Roman
←--- Roman withdrawal
← Carthaginian

0   50 miles
|——————————————|
0   50km

1. The Carthaginian armies are deployed separately, with Hasdrubal Barca's army to the east, and Mago Barca's men and Hasdrubal Gisco's army farther to the west near Castulo.
2. The Scipio brothers divide their forces. Publius Scipio is to attack Mago Barca near Castulo, while Gnaeus Scipio marches on Hasdrubal Barca near Ilorca. The resulting two battles are collectively known as the Battle of the Upper Baetis.
3. Hasdrubal Barca orders Iberian chieftain Indibilis and Hasdrubal Gisco to join Mago near Castulo.
4. Nearing Castulo, Publius Scipio is at risk of being surrounded by Carthaginian forces, and so at night attacks Indibilis, who is moving across his line of retreat.
5. The arrival of Mago and Hasdrubal Gisco leads to the Romans breaking and fleeing. Publius Scipio is killed.
6. Mago marches his forces towards Hasdrubal Barca's position.
7. Gnaeus Scipio, unaware of Publius Scipio's fate, withdraws at night towards northern Iberia. The Romans are forced to take up position on a hilltop north-east of Ilorca, which is overrun. Gnaeus is killed, and most of his army is destroyed.

While manoeuvring, the elder Scipio closed with the Suessetani the next day. The Iberians were ready to fight, perhaps knowing that their Punic allies would come to their aid. The problem for the elder Scipio was that the Romans had to fight in the order of their march, which suggests a column attack at least in the opening of the clash. Yet the consular army held the advantage because of their numbers and their discipline. With both forces using similar arms and armour, the clash was decided by the timely arrival of the Numidian cavalry. Masinissa's men had noticed the departure of the Roman legions, despite the care the Romans surely took to leave as silently as possible, cloaked by darkness. The Numidian light cavalry wreaked havoc on the wings, causing 'great terror' according to Livy. The Romans' fate was sealed by the arrival of Mago's Carthaginian infantry, having marched to the area after the Numidian cavalry had raced ahead to pin down the legion. Mago's African foot soldiers blocked the rear of the Roman army, sealing them in. The consular army was surrounded and was unable to effectively unite and fight in one direction to punch through one of the enemy's lines. In the midst of the desperate struggle, the elder Scipio was killed, run through by a lance in his right side by 'the party of the enemy, which, formed into a wedge, had charged the troops collected round the general'. Surrounded and leaderless, the dispirited Romans fled the field of battle, and even though they eventually managed to punch through the light-armed skirmishers and the Numidian cavalry on one side, they were soon caught out by the Punic-Iberian line infantry, skirmishers and cavalry, both line and light.

Typical Murcian countryside. It was in terrain very similar to this that Gnaeus Scipio made his last stand against the unified Carthaginian armies in 211 BC. His brother, the elder Scipio, had been killed a few weeks earlier. (Casasdeselva, CC-BY-SA 3.0 ES)

Livy records: 'Almost more were slain in the flight than in the battle; nor would a man have survived, had not night put a stop to the carnage.' Thus ended the life of the Roman leader who had made a strategic decision that ultimately saved Rome – sending his brother and the consular army to Iberia instead of to Italy was the decisive moment of the Second Punic War.

Castulo was a resounding victory for the Carthaginians, at a time when things had looked bleak for them in Iberia. However, the other half of the consular army under Gnaeus was still a threat. The victorious Punic-Iberian army marched without rest and in great haste towards Hasdrubal's army, hoping to unite all their field forces and force a conclusion to the war in Iberia by defeating Gnaeus and his remaining force. Doing so would enable Hasdrubal to march at long last to join his brother in Italy with reinforcements that had been denied Hannibal for six years by the Scipios' presence at Tarraco.

Gnaeus may not have heard the news of his brother's defeat and death but certainly the arrival of more Carthaginians indicated that somehow his brother had failed, either by retreat or defeat. The situation dictated a withdrawal to the north to join the elder Scipio's forces, or at worst any survivors. Gnaeus' Romans chose to march at night, hoping to avoid detection. They had covered a certain distance before Numidian cavalry discovered their presence, harassing the Roman rear columns and flanks – a typical Numidian cavalry tactic. The Romans had little choice but to defend themselves as best as possible and avoid being destroyed by a thousand cuts, as Livy notes: '[Gnaeus] exhorted them at once to fight so as not to expose themselves, and march at the same time, lest the infantry should overtake them.' Gnaeus understood the Punic tactic of using the Numidian light cavalry to pin down his force. There was little he could do as the skirmishing continued and slowed the Roman advance, but he was desperate to avoid the Carthaginian infantry that was in pursuit. Finally, Gnaeus ordered his men to withdraw and consolidate on a nearby hill, Monte Anaor, rising to an elevation of 186m, near the town of Ilorca. There, as Livy narrates, 'his infantry, drawn up around his baggage and cavalry, which were placed

THE UPPER BAETIS: THE BATTLE NEAR ILORCA, 211 BC (PP. 66–67)

Half the consular army was destroyed at the first battle of the Upper Baetis near Castulo, along with its commander the elder Scipio. The other half, under Gnaeus, was forced to retreat north at night, trying to hide their movement from the ever-present Numidian light cavalry. The following day, the Romans were caught and pinned in place by the cavalry, as more Punic forces began to arrive. Gnaeus opted to establish a defence, trying to avoid being cut to pieces while on the move. He withdrew his forces to a 186m hill called Monte Anaor, near the town of Ilorca. Here, he would face the combined might of three Carthaginian field forces as they closed in on his force.

In this scene, we see the ad hoc defence on the slopes of Monte Anaor ordered by Gnaeus. Unable to dig in due to the hard ground, the Romans have used wicker baskets and baggage train items to throw up a makeshift rampart. An unfinished section of the defensive barrier can be seen, while farther left a slightly more finished section has been constructed (**1**). The Roman soldiers have grabbed their weapons to face the growing mass of Carthaginians and their allies (**2**). Other Romans are seeking to escape by retreating up the slope, knowing they are outnumbered (**3**). All along the hill, soldiers, members of the baggage train and cavalry are manning the defences (**4**). The Numidian cavalry (**5**) have harassed and skirmished with the retreating Romans until Monte Anaor; now they have been joined by the veteran Punic line infantry (**6**). The trap is about to close shut around Gnaeus and his men.

in their centre, had no difficulty in repelling the attacks of the charging Numidians'. The hill was not so steep as to make the ascent difficult, and it featured a gentle rise towards the top. The problem for the Romans was the geography of their location. It did not allow the army to build a marching camp because the soil was too hard for digging. The hill itself was also bare of trees, so that no palisades could be cut. However, at least here they were able to reorganize and repel the Numidian cavalry attacks.

The key problem the Romans now faced was that they were on a hill and they lacked sufficient troops to face the three unified Carthaginian armies on the field of battle. Recognizing his disadvantage and desperate to improve his tactical situation, the battle-experienced Gnaeus ordered his men to build makeshift fortifications using wicker baskets heaped with baggage material.

According to Livy, the Carthaginian generals were initially contemptuous of these ad hoc defences, before realizing the difficulties involved in cutting through them to get at the Roman soldiers, who were fighting for their lives. It took time, but in the end the defences were breached and the Romans exposed to slaughter. Many had escaped into the forests and sought to make for the camp of the elder Scipio under the command of Titus Fonteius. How many legionaries escaped is unknown, given they were surrounded by so large a force and the superb Numidian cavalry and light skirmishers ready to kill fleeing soldiers who were streaming down and away from the hill. Some may have previously deserted as Gnaeus prepared his last stand. It seems unlikely that the location of the makeshift camp would have enabled many to escape. The legions were surrounded by jubilant Punic forces, killing who they could. Gnaeus, like his brother, died on Iberian soil, either slain once the assault had begun, or perhaps having escaped to a nearby fortified position which was in turn surrounded and then set on fire, captured and put to death. Livy records: '[Gnaeus] was slain in the eighth year after his arrival in Iberia, and on the 29th day after the death of his brother'.

Any Roman survivors of the two armies were now under the command of Fonteius, and made their way north of the Ebro. Under the leadership of the Roman *eques* Lucius Marcius Septimus, further desertion of Spanish tribes in the northern peninsula was prevented and the Roman forces of 8,000 foot and 1,000 horse consolidated and fortified their position. The Romans until then had undermined the loyalty of the Iberians to Carthage, but now they had suffered two enormous defeats and seen both commanders killed. Rome's hegemony was rolled back to the footprint it had previously occupied.

By 211/210 BC, Carthage retook lost ground south of the Ebro. Meanwhile in Italy, 12 out of 30 Latin colonies refused to send contingents to Rome. Things looked bleak for the Romans. In Iberia, they had lost all their gains south of the Ebro with the exception of Castulo and Saguntum. Hasdrubal stayed near the Ebro, where he detached Indibilis of the Ilergetae. Lucius Marcius along with Tiberius Fonteius and survivors from the twin battles and garrison troops from Emporion and Tarraco kept the Carthaginians from building a base north of the Ebro during the summer of 211 BC. In the autumn of 211 BC, a single new legion under two-year campaigning veteran Gaius Claudius Nero arrived in Iberia, and with elements from Lucius Marcius' forces formed the nucleus of a second legion, making up their losses from the previous year. Gaius Claudius was schooled in the strategy of delay first executed by Quintus Fabius Maximus Verrucosus against Hannibal.

A Roman gold coin struck around 211 BC in Rome, held at the Münzkabinett der Staatlichen Museen zu Berlin. The obverse shows the head of the god of war Mars, while the reverse shows an eagle with thunderbolts in its talons.

Throughout 210 BC, Gaius Claudius maintained a defensive strategy along the north-eastern seaboard. Hasdrubal, meanwhile, was certain he could not push Rome out of Emporion or Tarraco for lack of naval superiority. Instead, Hasdrubal focused on recruitment.

Roman concerns that a large army was to march overland to join Hannibal by 209 BC or the following year required offensive actions, and fortunately for Rome it had recaptured Capua (211 BC), Tarentum (209 BC) and other regions in Italy. Victory over Syracuse in Sicily allowed Rome to send two legions to Italy and have enough remaining power to deal with Iberia, while Carthage in Iberia managed only to regain lost territories. The war with Hannibal in Italy was deadlocked, slowly reversing the previously successful years. Iberia, on the other hand, proved to be the fulcrum on which the overall war pivoted: to the victor went the spoils.

THE YOUNGER SCIPIO AT NEW CARTHAGE, 209 BC

In 210 BC, the younger Scipio, whose father and uncle had been killed a year earlier, surprisingly replaced Gaius Claudius Nero. Along with Marcus Junius Silanus, he was sent with an additional 10,000 foot and 1,000 cavalry to Iberia to head up the by now four understrength legions of the consular army. The younger Scipio turned 25 upon appointment, a similar age to Hannibal when he had taken command of the Punic-Iberian army over a decade earlier. The younger Scipio was both a believer in the gods and in himself, as demonstrated by long vigils in prayer and his claim that his plan for the upcoming campaign was revealed to him in a dream by Neptune himself (his men adopted the battle cry of 'Neptunus dux itineris', 'Neptune leads the journey'). His fighting spirit, flexibility and understanding of Punic tactics made him a superb commander at a time when Rome was starting to experience success against Carthage.

Still, facing the younger Scipio were three Carthaginian armies spread throughout Iberia to offset logistics as well as to maintain control over the territories. Hasdrubal, son of Gisco, was near the mouth of the Tagus River (Livy says Gadir), Mago was far south near the Pillars of Hercules at Gibraltar (Livy gives Castulo) and Hasdrubal, brother of Hannibal, was in central Iberia in the lands of the Carpetani near the Tagus (Livy states Saguntum). All were at least a ten-day march from New Carthage. Each army probably numbered around 20,000 men.

The younger Scipio's siege of New Carthage, 209 BC

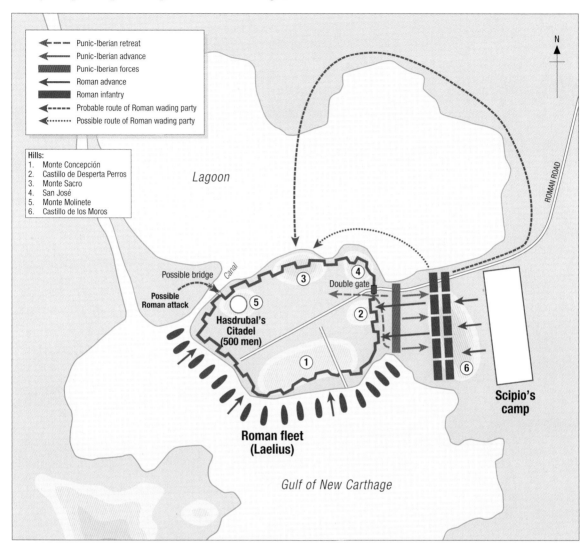

The challenge presented to the younger Scipio was the same his father and uncle had encountered. Fighting one army for too long would mean being pinned down in combat, risking the arrival of other Punic forces who would then unite and outnumber the consular army. Instead, his intelligence staff informed him of the strategic value of the Carthaginian stronghold New Carthage. According to Polybius, this centre of gravity determined his next move. The city was of tremendous value to the Carthaginian war effort with its natural harbour, the vast stores hoarded there supplying its military. Crucially, its small garrison numbered no more than 1,000 fighting men; the bulk of the population were craftsmen and fishermen unaccustomed to war. A lightning-fast and successful strike here at the heart of Punic Iberia would clearly favour the Romans and injure Carthaginian hegemony irreparably.

At the beginning of spring 209 BC, the younger Scipio assembled his legions and allies, 5,000 in number, at Tarraco and ordered his fleet to the mouth of the Ebro. Securing his interior lines of communication with 3,000

The ruins of the old city of New Carthage, Cartagena, Spain.

A view over the Gulf of Cartagena. One can see why Hasdrubal the Fair chose New Carthage for his base.

infantry and 300 cavalry under the command of Marcus Junius Silanus, the younger Scipio and his Roman-Iberian army of 25,000 foot and 2,500 horse crossed the Ebro. His fleet, under the command of his friend Gaius Laelius, was to assault New Carthage at the same time, approaching the harbour from the south.

New Carthage possessed impressive natural defences. The city was on a peninsula, running east to west, joined to the mainland on the east by a narrow piece of land; a sizeable lagoon lay to the north, connected to the sea to the south by an artificial canal to the west. Thus, the citadel was surrounded on three sides by water. The circuit of its walls ran for 3,700m and followed the steep, rocky slopes of five distinct hills, protected on all sides (except for the narrow isthmus) by the lagoon, the canal and Gulf of New Carthage. The city itself lay in lower ground, presenting on its southern side a level approach from the sea.

The younger Scipio pitched his camp on the eastern landward side of New Carthage, where the rear of the camp was protected by a double trench and rampart; on the side facing the town, it had no defences, for the nature of the ground made it sufficiently secure. It is highly questionable that the younger Scipio's consular army was able to cover the distance from Tarraco to New Carthage (590km) in seven days, as the ancient sources state – perhaps Saguntum was the correct origin, some 320km distant. Nonetheless, Scipio's legions arrived fast enough to avoid alerting the Carthaginian field forces. The same day, the fleet under Gaius Laelius began to lay siege to New Carthage from the south by blocking the neck of the gulf. The following morning, 2,000 of the strongest sailors accompanied the ladder-bearers and the assault began.

The New Carthage commander Mago (not Hannibal's brother) divided his forces into two groups, of 500 men each. One group was positioned at the citadel on the west, while the other was stationed on the eastern hill within the city. The civilian population provided 2,000 men at the gate to the isthmus facing the younger Scipio's camp. Other civilians were armed and tasked with manning the walls. Upon the Roman assembly and advance, the Carthaginians flowed out of the gate headlong into the assaulting force several hundred metres away. The defenders sought to delay the building of siege works and also to throw the Roman attack into disorder by

Cross section of a large boat exhibited in the National Museum of Underwater Archaeology, Cartagena, Spain. Note the relative size of the person on the left.

their surprise sally. A furious clash ensued, but the proximity to the Roman camp allowed the younger Scipio to feed more men into the battle until finally they pushed the Carthaginians back. Heavy casualties were suffered in the fighting, but Polybius states that greater numbers were trampled in their desperate flight back into the city. The terrified citizens abandoned the walls and the Romans nearly succeeded in breaching the gate and overcoming the walls with their ladders.

The next day, another Roman assault was driven back with heavy losses, but was followed up with two more assaults at noon and in the afternoon. The younger Scipio, according to Polybius, was in the thick of the action and managing the assault directly, protected by three men carrying large shields, inspiring his troops. The challenges facing the besiegers included the height of the walls, the fragility of the assault ladders bending beneath the weight of the troops and the beams and debris hurled onto the climbers from the defenders sweeping the Romans off the ladders. However, the zeal and fury, writes Polybius, of the Roman soldiers meant they replaced their fallen comrades and gained control of precious positions. At this point, and with the troops exhausted, the younger Scipio sounded the recall. No doubt the distant Hasdrubal was receiving alerts of the Roman siege by this stage.

The younger Scipio knew of the ebb and flow of the northern lagoon, and formed a plan. First, he urged new troops back into the assault against the eastern walls of New Carthage. With larger numbers and more ladders than before, the younger Scipio directed the twin assault against both the gate and the walls to the point where the entire facing walls had ladders leant against them. Detachment after detachment was sent into the fray. Meanwhile, the port of New Carthage was under blockade by the Roman fleet, perhaps launching missiles at the defenders and perhaps some assaults. While the Punic-Iberian defenders were fully engaged with these assaults, the younger Scipio sent 500 troops bearing ladders across the shallow water of the lagoon as the ebb of the tide began (the level of the sea near New

A modern reproduction of the Punic walls that surrounded New Carthage, Cartagena, Spain. Note the human figure, which gives an idea of the height of the walls climbed by the Romans during the siege.

Carthage, modern research shows, could drop by as much as 1.5m). These Romans climbed the undefended battlements of the northern walls, as Mago had insufficient troops to man the entire circumference, and moved east along them, engaging the defenders from the rear and sweeping them off the walls despite their spirited defence. The wading party probably came ashore somewhere between Monte Molinete and Monte Sacro; the defenders certainly did not expect a Roman assault from the lagoon side. No doubt there was so much disorderly shouting and confusion within the walls that the defenders could neither hear nor see what was occurring there. More and more of the walls fell under Roman control as Romans flooded into the city, driving the defenders away. The savagery displayed by the legions was horrific, Polybius tells us: 'not only human beings [were] put to the sword, but even dogs cloven down the middle, and the limbs of other animals hewn off. On this occasion the amount of such slaughter was exceedingly great, because of the numbers included in the city.'

The younger Scipio and some 1,000 soldiers advanced towards the citadel that was still held by Mago and his men. Seeing New Carthage in the hands of the dreaded enemy, Mago surrendered and the slaughter gave way to plunder. The war haul included massive amounts of military equipment and treasury most likely intended for Hannibal. Livy provides details of the astounding plunder: approximately 276lb of gold; 18,300lb of silver wrought and coined; and great numbers of silver vessels. There were 20,000 pecks of wheat and 270 of barley. Some 113 ships were boarded and captured in the harbour, some of them with their cargoes consisting of corn and arms, besides brass, iron, sails, rope/cable and other naval materials, of use in equipping a fleet. Roughly 600 talents of the Carthaginian war chest were added to the 400 the younger Scipio had for waging his campaign. Ten thousand free men were captured; the Carthaginians were allowed to depart with their property, while 2,000 craftsmen became the property of Rome with freedom offered should they support Rome in its war. The rest were inducted into the fleet as rowers to man the 18 captured warships. The Roman total now stood at 53 ships of war, all fully crewed. Among the weapons captured were 120 large catapults and 281 smaller ones, 23 large *ballistae* and 52 smaller ones, an immense number of large and small scorpions and missiles, and 74 military standards. Members of the Carthaginian senate, along with Mago, were also captured. The treasury of New Carthage along with ownership of the local silver mines provided Rome with more than enough funds to continue its expansion not only in Iberia but also throughout the Mediterranean. The Punic mint was captured; subsequently, coins with the Punic-style horse and palm tree on the reverse had Hannibal's portrait on the obverse replaced with that of the younger Scipio. Hostages were also taken from the Iberians.

With New Carthage under his control, the younger Scipio may have begun to retrain and rearm his troops while winning over local tribes, as his

Remains of the Punic walls at New Carthage, modern Cartagena, Spain.

father had previously done. The victory was a great morale boost for Rome, having been on the defensive for two years. Laelius was dispatched with prisoners to Rome, while the younger Scipio returned to Tarraco where he may have continued training his troops for the rest of the summer of 209 BC. North of the Ebro, the two kings of the Ilergetae, Indibilis and Mandonius, joined Rome. King Edesco of the Edetani, located between the Ebro and the Sucro, came to the Roman side as well.

The Carthaginians meanwhile still possessed three important river valley areas, providing agricultural and mineral wealth: the Tagus, Anas and Baetis. Hasdrubal now focused on raising new troops to join his brother Hannibal, though in hindsight the defence of Iberia was more valuable than providing support in Italy. Surrender was not in Hasdrubal's blood. Nonetheless, the fortunes of war had favoured the Romans and Hannibal needed help from his brothers if Carthage was to finally force Rome into a peace settlement.

A smaller vessel located at the National Museum of Underwater Archaeology, Cartagena, Spain. The younger Scipio probably captured a great many of these trading vessels after the fall of New Carthage.

THE BATTLE OF BAECULA, 208 BC

Hasdrubal's preparations to join Hannibal were monitored by the younger Scipio, who through a series of quick marches in the early spring of 208 BC sought a decisive battle. The clash took place at Baecula (near modern Santo Tomé, Jaén), according to archaeological evidence as well as ancient sources.

The Carthaginian camp at Baecula rested on the easternmost point of the Cerro de Las Albahacas, on the southern bank of the Baetis River some 278m above its bed. The camp was adapted to the terrain, with its longer axis facing north to south and its sides slightly curved. It was situated near an oppidum that sat north of the river. The camp provided an excellent view of the surrounding area and allowed for withdrawal north along the valley of the Baetis. It formed an excellent strategic position for Hasdrubal as it also prevented a Roman advance through the Baetis valley. The camp's defensive position was reinforced by entrenchments, large enough to allow for troop movements, and with pickets positioned at the edge of the hill.

The Roman camp was in the southern part of the Cerro de Las Albahacas. The younger Scipio's problem was that waiting for a battle to occur might provide enough time for other Carthaginian armies to surround him in a hammer and anvil scenario. After two days, he decided to launch an attack and test Hasdrubal's forces. Retaining the bulk of his army within the camp, he launched forward his *velites* and some picked men from the infantry to strike the enemy's pickets on the brow of the hill, as Polybius notes. The attack was furious, forcing Hasdrubal to deploy his army in support. This in turn led to the younger Scipio reinforcing the frontal assault with all of his light troops, while he advanced with half his army on the Roman right (the Carthaginian left flank); the other half, under Laelius, advanced on the Roman left, completing a pincer movement. We are told that these attacks caught Hasdrubal by surprise, and he was unable to deploy his army quickly thereby leaving his flanks exposed to the Roman advances on either side. The rushed movement of the Punic-Iberian units into battle formations led to confusion and disorder. The Romans exploited the confusion and killed some of the exposed men as they were falling in on the flanks, while others turned and fled (a common theme in Roman sources).

At this point, seeing his flanks melt away under pressure from the twin flank attacks and being pressed in his centre, Hasdrubal, according to Polybius, opted not to stake all on this one battle. The Carthaginian commander secured his treasury, his elephants (which seemed to have played no part in the engagement) and as many troops as he could muster and retreated northwards via the Baetis valley. The younger Scipio did not think it advisable to pursue Hasdrubal for fear of being attacked by the other Carthaginian generals, who must have been alerted to the battle. Instead, the Romans plundered Hasdrubal's camp.

Hasdrubal's force numbered nearly 25,000 to Scipio's 35,000–45,000, which included large numbers of the Ilergetae. Archaeological surveys as of yet have failed to locate any mass graves. The Roman victory was certainly not a resounding one despite the supposed capture of 12,000 prisoners.

The younger Scipio's army showed great tactical flexibility despite using the traditional triple-line formation. The consular army had two major weaknesses in general. First, although capable of advancing forwards and

The Battle of Baecula, 208 BC

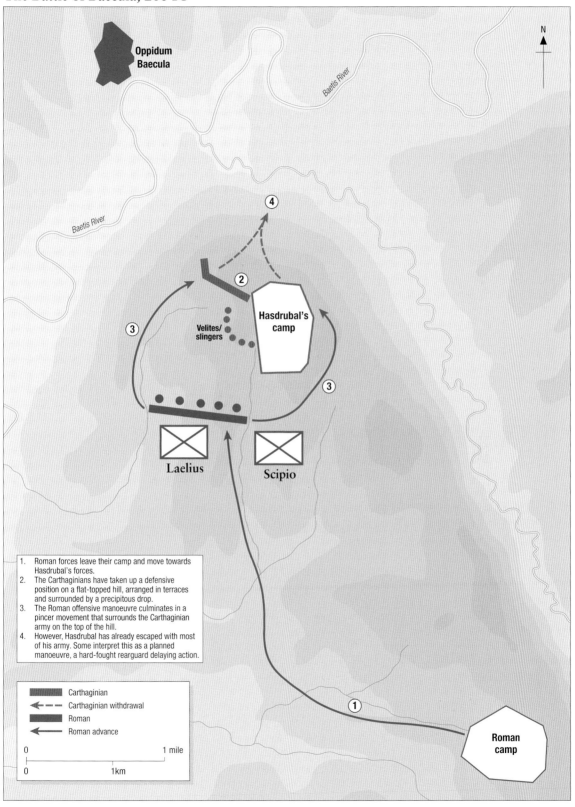

Oppidum
Baecula

Baetis River

N

Baetis River

4

2

3

Velites/
slingers

Hasdrubal's
camp

3

Laelius

Scipio

1. Roman forces leave their camp and move towards
   Hasdrubal's forces.
2. The Carthaginians have taken up a defensive
   position on a flat-topped hill, arranged in terraces
   and surrounded by a precipitous drop.
3. The Roman offensive manoeuvre culminates in a
   pincer movement that surrounds the Carthaginian
   army on the top of the hill.
4. However, Hasdrubal has already escaped with most
   of his army. Some interpret this as a planned
   manoeuvre, a hard-fought rearguard delaying action.

Carthaginian
Carthaginian withdrawal
Roman
Roman advance

0   1 mile
0   1km

1

Roman
camp

A masterpiece painted by the Italian Giovanni Battista Tiepolo (1696–1770) now exhibited at the Walters Art Museum, Baltimore, Ohio. It depicts the victorious younger Scipio freeing Masinissa's young nephew Massiva after the Battle of Baecula, ensuring Masinissa's loyalty to defeat Carthage.

backwards easily, it struggled to wheel itself or to face any flanking forces composed of fast-moving troops (as seen at the Battle of Cannae). Secondly, its rigid, basic training encouraged it to act as a single entity, leaving it incapable of independent movements by its maniples. The training after the capture of New Carthage of the Romans improved these limitations and led to greater success at Baecula.

Hasdrubal's decision to retreat north was a sound tactical one. The younger Scipio was unable to pursue the retreating army as he was in hostile land with stretched interior lines of communications and logistical support. Hasdrubal, however, had other plans and, reinforced by some of the other field forces, he moved from the Tagus north to cross the western Pyrenees and then marched through the Alps to join Hannibal in Italy at long last. His army cleverly avoided the Roman blocking forces dispatched along the eastern passes by the younger Scipio from the strongholds north of the Ebro by marching closer to the Atlantic seaboard. In many ways, this was a masterstroke by Hasdrubal. But having successfully crossed the Pyrenees and the Alps, in June 207 BC Hasdrubal would be killed at the Battle of the Metaurus in Italy.

Having failed to defeat Hasdrubal, the younger Scipio returned to Tarraco for winter quarters in 208/207 BC. Iberia was now exposed to an all-out attack from his forces. Carthage, recognizing the threat to the colony, sent yet another army, this time under Hanno, to join Mago's field force; the latter was busy recruiting Celt-Iberians at the beginning of 207 BC. Scipio's intelligence network reported the location where Hanno was training new recruits and dispatched Silanus with 10,000 troops. Silanus captured Hanno in a surprise attack, but Mago's main army withdrew to join the army of Hasdrubal, son of Gisco, at Gadir. The army of Hasdrubal, son of Gisco, mostly comprised inexperienced Iberian troops, unlike the younger Scipio's veteran force, and therefore it sought to avoid pitched battles. The younger

Scipio was allowed to lay siege to Iberian towns that refused to surrender. Central Iberia became devoid of Punic forces as native tribes switched allegiances, through use of force or diplomacy. The Iberian Peninsula was in a rapid transition from Punic to Roman.

An illustration by Bartolomeo Pinelli, dated around 1818, showing Hannibal receiving the severed head of his younger brother Hasdrubal, as instructed by the Roman commanders Marcus Livius Salinator and Gaius Claudius Nero following the Battle of the Metaurus in 207 BC.

THE BATTLE OF ILIPA, 206 BC

In 206 BC, the younger Scipio marched his forces from Castulo along the Baetis to face the unified army of Mago and Hasdrubal, son of Gisco, near Ilipa (Alcalá del Río, Sevilla). Here, a battle was fought between the modern villages of Esquivel and El Viar. Esquivel was built on the low plateau used by the Carthaginians (the outline of their camp is still visible), while El Viar was built adjacent to the elevations of the Roman encampment. Scipio encamped directly across from the Carthaginians. Both sides sought a decisive battle, aware of Hasdrubal's death the previous year at the Metaurus, which had forced Hannibal to abandon allied cities and to withdraw to Bruttium in southern Italy. The situation in the Italian theatre of war had now drastically tipped the balance of power in Rome's favour.

The Carthaginian forces were larger than those of the Romans. Hasdrubal, son of Gisco, and Mago may have had about 50,000 troops and 4,500 cavalry, although Polybius gives 70,000 foot, 4,000 horse and 32 (Livy says 36) elephants. The Punic-Iberian army was large because it collected men

A 16th-century etching by Antonio Fantuzzi (after Giulio Romano) showing slingers of the Roman army on the march. (The Met Museum)

along its way from the various towns used as winter quarters. They then marched to Ilipa, where they threw up a camp along with entrenchments at the foot of a hill facing a plain well suited for battle. Hasdrubal, son of Gisco, was in overall command. Qualitatively, however, the Punic army was not the same army that had conquered the Iberian Peninsula and defeated the Roman legions. The younger Scipio's veteran consular army had perhaps 40,000 in number, of which 25,000 were Roman soldiers, although Polybius lists it as having 45,000 infantry and 3,000 cavalry.

The first clash was a cavalry raid typical of Mago, who had proven his mettle in many battles and knew such raids were useful in unsettling enemy forces. The Punic cavalry, including Masinissa and his Numidians, charged the Roman encampment still under construction, but Roman and allied cavalry had been hidden in the cover of nearby higher ground to counter just such an attack. Mago's unit was repulsed after a heavy clash. It is surprising that Mago had not been aware of a possible ambush since he had used this tactic at the Battle of the Trebia in 218 BC, commanding a hidden force that had ambushed the Romans. Polybius writes: 'But the Carthaginians were disconcerted by the agility of some of the Roman horsemen in dismounting, and after a short resistance they retreated with considerable loss. The retreat was at first conducted in good order: but as the Romans pressed them hard, they broke up their squadrons, and fled for safety to their own camp.' It is doubtful that the agility of the Roman cavalryman made a difference. It seems more likely that, instead, the surprise attack coupled with an unknown number of Punic cavalry fleeing before the clash and the proximity of the Roman camp turned it in Rome's favour.

Over a number days, the armies drew up late in the afternoon fully knowing no battle would come, even though skirmishes involving cavalry and light-armed troops occurred. The younger Scipio usually formed his battle line after the Carthaginians deployed, which occurred late in the day. The order of battle of Hasdrubal, son of Gisco, featured the Libyan/African infantry in the centre, with Iberian allies on its wings supported by elephants. We assume the elephants were equally divided between the wings. The absence of cavalry is noteworthy. Perhaps they were on the wings in their traditional order. The central Roman battle line was composed of the consular army, while its wings were occupied by Iberian allies. Roman and allied cavalry were stationed on the wings in their traditional deployment.

The following morning, seeking battle, the younger Scipio demonstrated his tactical flexibility by reversing the order of the Roman battle line: he placed his allied Iberians in the centre and his Roman legions on the wings. He sent out harassing frontal attacks by his cavalry and light troops, forcing the Punic-Iberian army to hastily deploy in their traditional manner, but without breakfast we are told (a key factor in the eventual Roman victory, according to Polybius). The early-morning Roman battle deployment again caught the Carthaginian commanders off guard. They rushed their troops into formation on the plain – but now the best Roman soldiers faced the (according to Roman sources) weakest of the Carthaginian army, the Iberians on the wings. We should remember that this same kind of fighter had held the centre at the Battle of Cannae and fought valiantly for and against both Carthage and Rome.

The skirmishes to the front of the armies were fought resolutely between light-armed troops and cavalry. Many retreated to their main battle lines throughout the clashes. Eventually, the younger Scipio withdrew his skirmishers and his cavalry through the maniples on the wings and ordered the *velites* to take position in equal numbers behind each wing but in front of the cavalry. The entire Roman-Iberian army advanced in line for between one (Polybius) or five (Livy) stade – roughly between 185m and 925m. The latter is feasible as the distance between modern Esquivel and El Viar is just over 5km. At this point, the younger Scipio ordered his Iberian centre to continue the advance, while he ordered his Roman wings to march to the right and left respectively (leaving massive gaps in the line of battle) and the allied Iberians to continue to push forwards. He commanded the right wing, while Lucius Marcius and Marcus Junius led the left. The younger Scipio may have joined the right wing during latter stages of the battle, ensuring the execution of his orders on the left first. It seems the movements most likely were accomplished by facing manoeuvres and then simply marching in column forwards, thereby also reducing their vulnerability to missiles. At a certain point, the Roman line extended just past that of the Carthaginians. Here, they then executed another manoeuvre and fell into line by wheeling into traditional battle formation with the cavalry at the extreme ends, facing the Carthaginian elephants. The Roman movement was interesting: the right and left wings did everything in opposite directions, with the cavalry turning half-right and the infantry turning half-left on the right wing, and vice versa on the left wing. This meant they now concentrated their wings against the extreme end of the Punic lines filled with the weaker Iberian troops. We presume the Roman and allied cavalry (although stationed behind the light-armed troops and the maniples of infantry originally) now occupied the extreme ends of the Roman wings with the *velites*, because cavalry and light-armed men move faster than heavy shield-carrying infantry and could

THE BATTLE OF ILIPA, 206 BC (PP. 82–83)

Here, we see parts of the far left wing of the Carthaginian army during the very early stages of the battle. The younger Scipio has quickly deployed his army first and in reverse order, catching the Punic army off guard. On the far left wing, elephants and skirmishers, still extending farther to the left, are caught out by the rapidly approaching Roman cavalry, accompanied by *velites* (skirmishers), representing the Roman far right, while the rest of the Roman legion infantry is now deploying into formation ready to attack the disorganized Iberian line troops. The Punic cavalry is strangely absent, even though they have been present in earlier skirmishes. The Roman right wing under the younger Scipio is starting to unfold, revealing line infantry (**1**), cavalry (**2**) and *velites* (**3**). To the right of the Carthaginian elephants we see the outer edge of the Punic-allied Iberian fighters in open formation (**4**), representing the left wing of the Carthaginian army. Instead of having other native troops facing them, they now must fight the best of the consular army. The African troops stationed in the centre are pinned by Rome's Iberian allies and are thus unable to counter-move. The younger Scipio's reverse formation, with Romans on the wings instead of in the centre, will pay dividends in this battle.

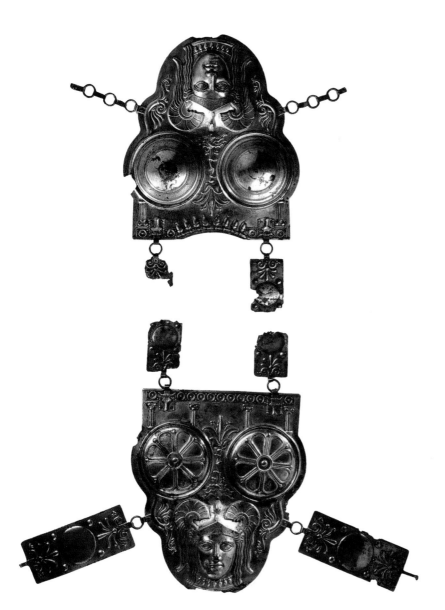

The Ksour Essef bronze cuirass, composed of a breastplate and a backplate decorated with the helmeted head of the Roman goddess Minerva. Its precise age is uncertain, ranging from the end of the 2nd to the 1st century BC. Although found in Tunisia, it is thought to have come from southern Italy.

more easily envelop slow-moving infantry or deal with enemy horsemen when required on the flanks. The question is: what happened to the two excellent Punic cavalry commanders, Mago and Masinissa? Both were experienced leaders, and we know they were at the battle, but seemingly they were incapable of rising to the occasion by charging into the gaps left by the Roman manoeuvres. Exploiting those holes could easily have led to the destruction of the Roman allied Iberian centre, or they might have been able to isolate one of the Roman wings by either harassing them (thereby delaying their advance and allowing the Carthaginian infantry to redeploy) or with luck driving the Romans from the field.

The Roman wings advanced in line while the allied Iberian centre advanced more slowly, pinning the opposing African centre and leaving them unable to move. The battle was now fully in the seventh hour of the day according to Livy. The Roman and allied cavalry, assisted by the *velites*,

Note: gridlines are shown at intervals of 1km (0.62 miles)

CARTHAGINIAN
50,000–70,000 infantry
A. Celt-Iberians and Iberians
B. Libyans/Africans
C. 32–38 elephants

xxxx

YOUNGER SCIPIO

BATTLE OF ILIPA, 206 BC

At Ilipa, the Roman victory was achieved through the adoption of Hannibalian tactics by Scipio, who used a double-flanking manoeuvre to bring about an emphatic Roman victory in Spain.

EVENTS

Phase 1

1. Late in the day before the battle, the younger Scipio formed his battle line after the Carthaginians deployed. The central Roman battle line is composed of the consular army and its wings are occupied by Iberian allies together with the Roman and allied cavalry. However, on the morning of the battle, the younger Scipio switches his allied Iberians into the centre while his Roman legions form the wings. His best soldiers are thus facing the weakest of the Carthaginian army – the Iberians on the wings. The younger Scipio sends out harassing frontal attacks by his cavalry and light troops.

Phase 2

2. The younger Scipio withdraws his skirmishers, including his cavalry, through the maniples on the wings and orders the *velites* in equal numbers behind each wing but in front of the cavalry. The entire Roman-Iberian army advances in line.

3. The younger Scipio orders his Iberian centre to continue the advance while his Roman wings march to the right and left respectively in columns, leaving massive gaps in the line of battle as the allied Iberians still march forward.

4. When the Roman line extends past that of the Carthaginians, they execute another manoeuvre and fall into line by wheeling into traditional battle formation with the cavalry on the extreme ends, facing the elephants.

5. The Roman wings advance in line while the allied Iberian centre advances more slowly, pinning the opposing African centre into frozen ground, unable to move. The battle is now in the seventh hour of the day according to Livy.

Phase 3

6. The Roman and allied cavalry, along with the *velites*, maul the Carthaginian elephants and skirmishers, causing enormous destruction to both sides. The Carthaginian flanks are eventually crushed by the sheer numbers and strength of the Roman legions around midday.

7. The African centre remains pinned in place by the threat to the Roman-allied Iberians to their front, unable to fight or move.

8. Although the Roman wings are successful, they fail to meet in the middle to win a resounding victory. The Carthaginians are able to retreat in an orderly fashion to their camp, which they fortify.

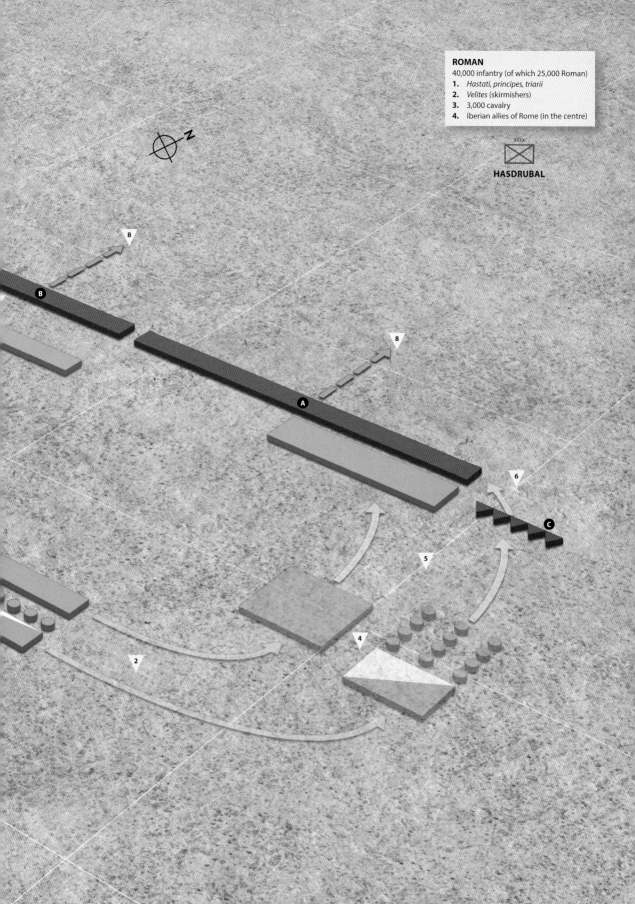

ROMAN
40,000 infantry (of which 25,000 Roman)
1. *Hastati, principes, triarii*
2. *Velites* (skirmishers)
3. 3,000 cavalry
4. Iberian allies of Rome (in the centre)

HASDRUBAL

mauled the elephants causing enormous destruction to both sides as the maddened animals desperately tried to escape their human tormenters. We presume Punic and Iberian light troops supported the elephants on the wings, holding their own until they were eventually crushed by the sheer numbers and strength of the Roman legions around midday.

The African centre, pinned in place by the threat to the Roman-allied Iberians to their front, was unable to contribute to the battle. Yet one wonders why the African centre did not press forwards to punch a hole into their opposing line? Fear of the Roman wings could be one explanation, but that would mean their own Punic-allied Iberians on the wings would have remained in place, in case the Roman wings had to turn prematurely to deal with the advancing African line. The absence of the Punic-Iberian cavalry forces is startling, as is the lack of counter-measures employed by the Carthaginian leadership. The Carthaginian cavalry that was present may have been disordered or dispersed by their own elephants. Surely, Mago and Masinissa would have remembered the battles they fought in Italy, where large numbers of Romans punched through their lines escaping the Punic death trap set at the Trebia, and where not going through the centre caused mass casualties at Cannae. Punching through the thinly manned Roman-Iberian centre would have guaranteed some success, or at least another outcome. Although the Roman wings were successful, they never managed to meet in the middle to win a resounding victory, as Hannibal had done 12 years earlier at Cannae. It was an unfinished masterpiece as the Carthaginians retreated in an orderly fashion without incurring catastrophic losses. Perhaps the lack of a sizeable Roman cavalry element allowed the African and Iberian survivors to withdraw to their camp, which they reinforced with stonework from the immediate area. Livy states: 'Had not Providence interfered to save them, they would promptly have been driven from their camp, too; but a sudden storm gathered in the air, and a violent and prolonged torrent of rain descended, under which the Romans with difficulty effected a return to their own camp ... Many Romans [also] lost their lives by the fire in trying to get the silver and gold which had been melted and fused.' Iberian desertions did occur from the Punic side, according to Livy, including one 'Attenes, prince of the Turdetani, who deserted with a large force of his tribesmen'; and 'two fortified towns were handed over with their garrisons to the Romans by their commanders'.

The following night, Hasdrubal, son of Gisco, moved his camp. This seemed to occur without Roman interference. Eventually, the Carthaginians retreated to the coast, where Hasdrubal, son of Gisco, Mago and the remnants of their army withdrew separately by sea. Livy writes of 6,000 survivors by the time Hasdrubal, son of Gisco, made his escape to Carthage.

The Battle of Ilipa was a Roman victory based on Hannibalian tactics adopted by Scipio. The double-flanking movement by the Roman consular army displaced the last major Carthaginian field force and ensured a Roman victory in Iberia. Ancient sources tend to glorify Scipio's genius because of his tactics, yet other commanders, Carthaginian and Roman, also used tactical flexibility and ingenuity to defeat opposing armies. Out of all the opposing commanders, perhaps no one was greater than Hannibal during the Second Punic War.

AFTERMATH

ROME SECURES IBERIA

The exploitation of the victory at Ilipa was more emphatic for the younger Scipio than the actual battle. Subsequent smaller battles and skirmishes both on land and sea saw further Roman victories. A few fortresses and tribes were subjugated, but no Carthaginian army returned to challenge for Iberia again. The younger Scipio sent his brother Lucius to conquer the Oretani in the mining region around Castulo, while a Roman force

The inside of a Renaissance pageant shield painted on both the interior and exterior. The battlescenes on the inside of this shield perhaps illustrate episodes from the life of the younger Scipio. Dated to 1535 by Italian sculptor and painter Girolamo da Treviso (1498–1544). (The Met Museum)

seized several towns. Some residents of the towns fought to the last, others surrendered. Gadir, where Mago was in command prior to his final retreat, frustrated attempts by Scipio and Laelius, commanding the navy, to seize the town by treachery. The Roman fleet sailed back to New Carthage.

At New Carthage, news emerged that the troublesome Iberian leaders Indibilis and Mandonius had rebelled while the younger Scipio was ill (rumour had it seriously so), leading to the mutiny of garrison troops at Sucro. Having brutally put down the mutiny, the younger Scipio again busied himself subduing tribes.

During the younger Scipio's campaign north of the Ebro, and fully recognizing that Gadir would eventually be taken, Mago seized the initiative and attacked New Carthage. Mago's attack failed, however, and upon his return to Gadir the gates were shut to him (supposedly because his solders had looted before leaving the city); Mago then executed several of the Gadir envoys sent to negotiate with him. Surrendering to Rome was unacceptable and Mago with his small army sailed to the capital named after him, Minorca (Mahón) in the Balearic Islands.

The younger Scipio met with the Numidian Masinissa, and the latter decided to join in alliance with Rome. This eventually came to full effect when Numidian cavalry played the key role in Hannibal's defeat at the Battle of Zama in 202 BC.

Iberia's mineral wealth was transferred to aid the Roman war machine. By 205 BC, the younger Scipio, with Marcius and Silanus now in command, and after having founded the first Roman city in Iberia (Italica), travelled to Rome seeking a consulship.

AFTERMATH

The war in the Iberian Peninsula was effectively over, but Mago Barca was not a man to quit. Instead, in 205 BC he sailed with the remnants of his army to Liguria after having stopped in the Balearic Islands. His 15,000 men and 30 ships captured Genoa in Italy, and from there he moved into Cisalpine Gaul. The following year he received not only reinforcements from Carthage in the form of 6,000–7,000 infantry and an unknown number of cavalry and a handful of elephants, but also in the form of many Celts (Gauls): '[Mago's] army grew in numbers every day; the Gauls, drawn by the spell of his name, flocked to him from all parts.' Mago tied up seven Roman legions for three years. The Romans' tactic was to block his advance to reinforce Hannibal, who was by now on the defensive after nearly 14 years campaigning in mainland Italy.

In 203 BC, Mago's Punic-Iberian-Celt army of perhaps 20,000 veterans and several thousand Celts faced four Roman legions, perhaps 30,000, at the Battle of Insubria in north-western Italy, near Milan. The Romans deployed two legions to the front, while the other two legions along with the cavalry remained in reserve. Mago deployed his forces, but kept the Celts and elephants behind his lines. The Punic army clashed heavily with the Roman line and Roman cavalry, which had been brought forward to disorder the Carthaginian lines, but Mago's timely use of his elephants dispersed the Roman horses, as Livy recounts:

> Terrified by their roar and odour and by the sight of them, the horses made the assistance of the cavalry useless. And although, so long as they were in the thick of the fight, where they could make use of the lance and, at close quarters, of the sword, the Roman horsemen were the stronger, still when they were carried to a distance by frightened horses, the Numidians were the more successful in hurling javelins from a longer range.

Livy states the elephant charge supported by the Numidians also severely mauled the Roman infantry of the XII Legion. Only the timely arrival of the second line of the XIII Legion reestablished order. The elephants were routed by the *hastati* of the XI Legion, leaving behind four disabled ones, the rest driven back to the Punic lines, wreaking havoc as Mago had pushed his Celts forward. But Mago's allies fought valiantly, even though they were being pushed back slowly. Inspired by Mago's presence, they stayed in the battle until at one point Mago was wounded in his thigh (like Hannibal at Saguntum), causing panic and disorder among his Celtic reserve. The battle was over, but it was a close-run thing, as Livy describes:

> Two thousand three hundred were lost from the army of the praetor, much the larger part of them from the XII Legion; from it also two tribunes of the soldiers, Marcus Cosconius and Marcus Maevius. Of the XIII Legion also, which had taken part in the last phase of the battle, Gaius Helvius, tribune of the soldiers, fell while rallying the men. And about 22 knights of the

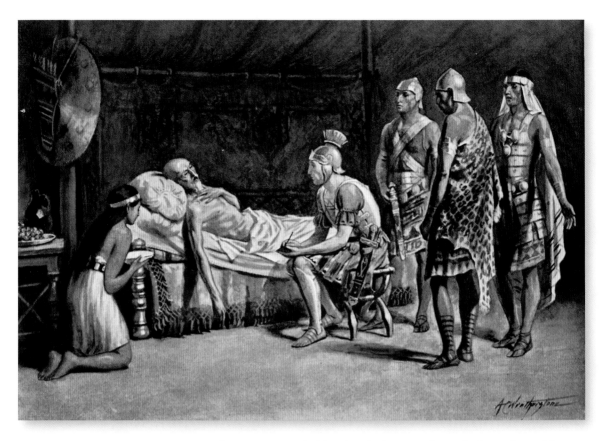

Scipio Aemilianus (185–129 BC) at the deathbed of Masinissa (c.240–148 BC) by Alfred C. Weatherstone (1888–1929).

upper class were trampled by the elephants and perished together with a number of centurions. Also the engagement would have lasted even longer, had not victory been conceded because of the general's wound.

Mago's army marched at night and throughout the following days through Ligurian lands of the Ingauni. He received Punic envoys in Genoa recalling him to Carthage, where the Romans had won two tremendous victories. Mago Barca, according to Livy, died of his wounds near Sardinia on his way home to join Hannibal in North Africa.

The Battle of Insubria represented the dying embers of the war for Carthage. Hannibal was defeated the following year at the Battle of Zama, where his inferior army was defeated by the younger Scipio and Masinissa's Numidians. The Second Punic War was over.

SELECT BIBLIOGRAPHY

Primary sources

Appian, *Wars in Spain*, https://www.perseus.tufts.edu/hopper/text?doc=Perseus:text:1999.01.0230:text=Hisp.:chapter=7

Diodorus, *Fragments*, https://penelope.uchicago.edu/Thayer/E/Roman/Texts/Diodorus_Siculus/25*.html

Frontinus, *The Stratagems*, II, ii.14–iii.2, https://archive.org/details/sextus-julius-frontinus-the-stratagems-and-aqueducts-of-rome-translated-by-charles.-e.-bennett/page/106/mode/2up

Livy, *History of Rome*, https://www.perseus.tufts.edu/hopper/text?doc=Perseus%3Atext%3A1999.02.0166%3Abook%3D38

Nepos, Cornelius, *Lives of Eminent Commanders*, XXIII. *Hannibal*, https://tertullian.org/fathers/nepos.htm#Hamilcar

Plutarch, *The Parallel Lives*, *The Life of Romulus*, https://penelope.uchicago.edu/Thayer/E/Roman/Texts/Plutarch/Lives/Romulus*.html

Polybius, *Histories*, https://www.perseus.tufts.edu/hopper/text?doc=Perseus%3atext%3a1999.01.0234

Secondary sources

Bellón, Juan Pedro, Carmen Rueda, Miguel Ángel Lechuga and María Isabel Moreno, 'An Archaeological Analysis of a Battlefield of the Second Punic War: The Camps of the Battle of Baecula', *Journal of Roman Archaeology*, 29, 2016

Ben Khader, Aicha Ben Abed, Hedi Slim and David Soren, *Carthage: From the Legends of The Aeneid to the Glorious Age of Gold – An Engrossing History of the Vanished Empire that Rivaled Athens and Rome*, Touchstone, New York, 1990

Cary, M. and H.H. Scullard, *A History of Rome*, 3rd Edition, St Martin's, New York, 1983

Castro, José Luis López, 'The Iberian Peninsula' in *The Oxford Handbook of the Phoenician and Punic Mediterranean*, Oxford University Press, Oxford and New York, 2019 (pp. 584–602)

Cook, S.A., F.E. Adcock, M.P. Charlesworth and N.H. Baynes (eds), *The Cambridge Ancient History*, Vol. VIII: *Rome and the Mediterranean 218–133 BC*, Cambridge University Press, Cambridge, 1930 (reprinted 1981)

Dobson, Michael, *The Army of the Roman Republic: The Second Century BC, Polybius and the Camps at Numantia, Spain*, Oxbow Books, Oxford, 2008

Hoyos, Dexter, *Unplanned Wars*, De Gruyter, Berlin, 1998

—— (ed.), *A Companion to the Punic Wars*, Wiley-Blackwell, Oxford, 2011

——, *Mastering the West*, Oxford University Press, Oxford and New York, 2015

——, *Carthage's Other Wars: Carthaginian Warfare Outside the Punic Wars Against Rome*, Pen & Sword Military, Barnsley, 2019

Fields, Nic, *The Roman Army in the Punic Wars 264–146 BC*, Osprey Publishing, Oxford, 2007

Hill, Andrew, 'Hamilcar of Barce? Discerning Barcid Proto-history and Polybius' Mixellēnes', *The Journal of Hellenic Studies*, 140, 2020

Ilevbare, J.A., *Carthage, Rome and the Berbers*, Ibadan University Press, Ibadan, 1981

Lancel, Serge, *Carthage: A History*, Blackwell Publishers, Oxford, 1997

Lazenby, John, *The First Punic War*, Stanford University Press, Stanford, 1996

——, *Hannibal's War*, University of Oklahoma Press, Norman, 1998

MacDonald, Eve, *Hannibal: A Hellenistic Life*, Yale University Press, New Haven, 2015

Montenegro, J. and A. Del Castillo, 'Some Reflections on Hamilcar Barca and the Foundation of Acra Leuce', *Athenaeum*, Vol. 105, II, 2017

Morrison, J.S., *Greek and Roman Oared Warships 399–30 BC*, Oxbow Monograph 62, Oxford, 2016

Noguera, Jaume, 'La Palma – Nova Classis. A Publius Cornelius Scipio Africanus Encampment during the Second Punic War in Iberia', *Madrider Mitteilungen*, 53, VIII, 2012

Picard, Gilbert and Colette Picard, *Carthage*, Sidgwick & Jackson, London, 1987

Rodgers, William Ledyard, *Greek and Roman Naval Warfare*, Naval Institute Press, Maryland, 1964

Sanz, Fernando Quesada, 'Not so Different: Individual Fighting Techniques and Small Unit Tactics of Roman and Iberian Armies', *Pallas*, 70, 2006

——, 'Iberians as Enemies' in *Encyclopedia of the Roman Army*, Vol. I, Wiley-Blackwell, Oxford, 2015

Scullard, H.H., *Scipio Africanus: Soldier and Politician*, Cornell University Press, New York, 1979

——, 'The Carthaginians in Spain' in *The Cambridge Ancient History*, Cambridge University Press, 1989

Taylor, Michael James, *Finance, Manpower, and the Rise of Rome*, PhD dissertation, University of California, Berkeley, 2015

——, *Soldiers and Silver: Mobilizing Resources in the Age of Roman Conquest*, University of Texas Press, Austin, 2020.

Tipps, G.K., 'The Rogum Scipionis and Gnaeus Scipio's Last Stand', *The Classical World*, Vol. 85, No. 2, November–December 1991

Treuman-Watkins, Brigitte, 'Phoenicians in Spain', *The Biblical Archaeologist*, Vol. 55, No. 1, March 1992

Walbank, F.W., *Polybius: A Historical Commentary on Polybius*, 3 vols, Oxford University Press, Oxford, 1967–70

INDEX

References to illustrations and information in captions are shown in **bold**